Windfalls

Preserves and Other
Country Kitchen Secrets

SUE RUCHEL

Aird Books

MELBOURNE

For Virginia and her sisters

Manna Trading Pty Ltd
PO Box 122
Flemington, Vic. 3031
Phone (03) 9376 4461

First published by Aird Books (an imprint of Manna Trading) in 1993
Reprinted with corrections 2007

National Library of Australia
Cataloguing-in-publication data

Ruchel, Sue, 1931
    Windfalls: preserves and other country kitchen secrets.
    Includes index. ISBN 9780947 2144 87

    1.Cookery (Fruit). 2. Jam. 3. Fruit-Preservation. I. Title. 641.64

Cover design and illustration by Helen Semmler
Text design and illustrations by Helen Semmler
Typeset in-house by Aird Books
Printed by Everbest, China

The author and 'Tumbler's Green'

Sue Ruchel grew up among the apple and pear orchards which once ringed Melbourne. For many years she lived on a farm in the Victorian Mallee, then, later, on the Central coast of New South Wales and on a tropical island in the Pacific.

Now Sue has settled down in a small and beautiful house in a large and beautiful garden called 'Tumbler's Green' in the highlands of Central Victoria, from where she works as a writer and professional gardener and cook.

$\mathcal{C}$ontents

Acknowledgments

When I was a young wife who knew little of cooking I had a wonderful neighbour on the next property whom I could phone for help with my very amateurish attempts at jam, sauce and pickle making. Her name is Mrs Schilling. She is a very old lady now but thanks to her, and to my mother, my grandmother, and many other friendly cooks I have known, I eventually learnt how to cook.

Good cooks are usually happy to share their skills and pass on recipes and I would like to thank all my friends and family and the unknown cooks and cookery writers, whose recipes I have collected over the years. Without them this book would not have been written, my family would not have been fed so well, and my daughters would not have grown up to be the wonderful cooks they are. I would like to thank Caroline and Jenny at Australian Literary Management for their generous help and encouragement.

I gratefully acknowledge the co-operation of the poets, owners of copyright and publishers who have given permission for poems to appear in this book. They are: Angus & Robertson for 'Mallee in October' by Flexmore Hudson and 'Song of the Rain' by Hugh McRae; Kate Llewellyn for 'Figs', 'Lemons' and an excerpt from 'Quinces' (and her mother's fig jam recipe); Richard Tipping for 'Mangoes'; Susan Perry for 'Shelling Peas'; and Lothian Publishing for the excerpt from 'Victoria Markets Recollected in Tranquillity' by Furnley Maurice (F J Wilmot).

Most of all I thank my strong and beautiful daughter Virginia for the enormous amount of practical help and encouragement she has given me with this book.

Cooking Terms

I have tried to make the instructions simple and straightforward but there may be some terms with which you are unfamiliar.

Blanching   The process of pouring boiling water (sometimes salted) over vegetables or fruit before pickling.

Boiling   Fluids reach boiling point at 100°C. Most jams set at 104°C, so to boil briskly and bring the jam to setting point the temperature must be a little more than boiling. The mixture will need to boil hard to achieve this.

Brine   Brine is made from water and salt and is used for soaking vegetables before cooking. Use 50 g salt for 5 L of water or according to taste.

Cream of Tartar, Tartaric Acid and Citric Acid   These are usually available in supermarkets.

Jelly Bag   Jelly bags are made from muslin or cheesecloth, which can be bought cheaply from most fabric shops, and are used to strain the fruit to create a clear jelly.

Pectin   This is the substance present in fruit which makes the jam set when the correct amount of sugar is added and heat is applied. Some fruits have plenty of pectin; some may need the addition of acid to help it set. Lemon juice is a good source of acid.

Sealing   If the mixture is hot enough when bottled and lids are applied and screwed down quickly the bottle will most likely seal itself from the steam off the surface of the preserve. If a more enduring seal is needed jars can be steam-sealed by being placed in a pan of water with the lids on and brought to the boil. This steam will seal the lids securely. If you stand the jars on a metal surface they will break so use a wooden stand in the bottom of the pan (an old breadboard will do) or a wad of folded paper. Keep the lid on the pan.I found when I lived in a hot climate I needed to steam seal almost everything. Here in the cool highlands I hardly ever need to do it.

Setting test/point   The easiest setting test is the saucer test. Place a spoonful of jam on a saucer and cool it rapidly. I keep a corner of the freezer section of the refrigerator clear and just put it in for a minute. Tilt the saucer and if the jam wrinkles like the skin of hot milk it is ready.

If you have a sugar thermometer check the temperature of the jam. Most jams and jellies set at $104^{\circ}C$. I would still use the saucer test as a double check.

Simmer   This means to bring the liquid to just below boiling point and maintain that temperature for the period of cooking.

Skimming   Scum rises to the surface of jam when it is cooking and this should be lifted off with a slotted spoon before the jam is bottled.

Sodium metabisulphite or Milton solution or tablets   These are available from chemists for sterilising jars and bottles.

Sterilise   To destroy bacteria and other living (micro-) organisms by heating in boiling water, steam or dry heat, or by using a chemical solution like sodium metabisulphite as described above.

Introduction

I decided I had to write this book one tranquil morning as I picked blackberries in a sunny corner of the golf links beside my house. Tiny firetail finches whirred through the bushes, unafraid of me or my fat, short-legged dog as she nosed about in the undergrowth. The morning was crisp and humming with silence. The sun was warm on my back. My snake boots and old shirt made getting the fattest blackberries in the middle of the bushes a breeze. My bucket filled with ridiculous ease. It was a morning for the memory box.

I thought of my hard-working children and young friends, juggling their jobs and families, who will never have time to go blackberrying on a weekday morning. I wanted to hold the day and give it to them as a special gift. I would go home in a short time and spend the rest of the day making jams, jelly and blackberry pies and there would still be some left over for the freezer.

How could I pass on to them the pleasure and satisfaction such simple unsophisticated pastimes bring? I knew I had to write it all down for them in an uncomplicated, quick and easy way, so this is a very personal book.

I grew up among the apple and pear orchards which once ringed Melbourne. I lived for many years on a farm in the Victorian Mallee, then later on the Central Coast of New South Wales and on a tropical island in the Pacific. Now I live in a small and beautiful house in a large and beautiful garden called 'Tumbler's Green' in the cool highlands of Central Victoria.

In all these places I have had beautiful and productive gardens. I have cooked and made jams, jellies and pickles and collected recipes. I have found things to do with a million chokos from the back fence (they come only in millions) and have made jam with everything from pawpaws and mangoes to cherries and quandongs.

I cannot claim this to be an indigenous Australian cookbook. The only Australian plants I have used are the lilly pilly and quandong, those fruits so valued by the first Australians and people like my husband, who looks for his quandong pies and jam every spring. There are lilly pilly trees in gardens, bushland and street plantings, especially in Melbourne, and quandongs grow all over the dry inland of Australia.

Like the people of Australia almost all the food-producing plants we commonly use have come from somewhere else. Like the people, they have acclimatised and thrived, so much so that we now take for granted one of the best and cheapest supplies of fresh fruit and vegetables in the world.

Basic recipes for making jams, jellies and pickles do not vary greatly so there is nothing startlingly new or different here. My aim is to pass on simple, quick methods and the feeling of magic and satisfaction that comes from creating something special from readily available and often wasted produce. You certainly don't need a garden to use this book. Fruit is always cheap in season, and the markets, roadside fruit stalls and even your friendly neighbourhood greengrocer are great sources of raw materials. My greengrocer saves me the over-ripe mangoes, strawberries, raspberries and even starfruit and rhubarb which I make into jams or whatever. I take him a jar of something from each batch. We are both happy with that arrangement.

'Pick-your-own' places are a great family day out. Kids are mostly allowed to eat as much as they like, and to go home to berries or cherries and cream makes it really special. Many PYO places sell their produce frozen or fresh and it is always available. It costs more to buy them picked but if time is short it is the only way. There is no better way of spending a summer day than at a PYO farm. Even a couple of punnets of strawberries or a kilo of plums from a fruit barrow on the way home from work is enough to get you going with pickling and preserving.

I have purposely made the recipes for small quantities. Preserves set better, have a better colour, and the cutting up and cooking of small amounts is a pleasant rather than a wearisome task. If you want to make a bigger batch than specified just double the quantities but remember to double the cooking time too. Fruit and vegetables can be frozen in weighed portions to be cooked at another time. On a winter day when it's too wet to do anything else the whole family can enjoy a 'jam session' and the warm jammy smell filling the house will remind them that summer will come again.

Most of the recipes are in weighed or measured quantities. It is sometimes easier to use cup and spoon measures and I have done this where it seems logical. An ordinary breakfast cup holds 220 g of solids and 200 mL of liquid. All spoon measures are level.

A quarter of a teaspoon equals $1 \frac{1}{4}$ mL, half a teaspoon equals $2 \frac{1}{2}$ mL, one teaspoon equals 5 mL, and one tablespoon equals 20 mL. Measures are based on these amounts.

I hope you will enjoy trying my 'Windfall' recipes. They are quick and easy to cook. I have included some soul food for you too – some of my favourite Australian poems to read while you are stirring or watching the pot.

Good stirring, good cooking and good eating.

Sue Ruchel
'Tumblers Green', Creswick 1993

Cheap today lady; cheap today!
Jostling water melons roll
from fountains of Earth's mothering soul,
Tumbling from box and tray
Rosy, cascading apples play
Each with a glowing auriole
Caught from a spilt sunray. Cheap today lady; cheap
Cheap today lady; cheap today.

   . . . from the throbbing mart
Go cheese and celery, pears and jam
In barrow, basket, bag or pram
To the last dram the purse affords
Food, food for the hordes.

Pouring sun, pouring heavens, pouring earth,
And the life giving seas:
Treasure eternally flowing forth,
None greater than these!
Richness, colour and form.
Ripe flavours and juices rare.

Excerpts from *The Victoria Markets Recollected in Tranquillity*
by Furnley Maurice (F J Wilmot)

CHAPTER ONE

Getting it all together

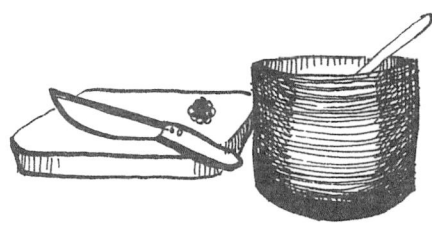

Kissin don't last, cookin do.
(Old saying)

When my mother and grandmother made jam it took them a whole day. My mother had huge copper and aluminium preserving pans that she would watch like a hawk once jam making began. She made huge quantities at a time and it always seemed to be a the hottest time of the year.

It is no longer necessary to spend long days slaving over a hot stove in 30 degree heat to make jams and pickles. You can make them in small quantities in a short time when fruit is ripe or the vegetables are cheap in the market. You can also freeze some of the produce to make more jams and pickles when you have time and the weather is cooler. I find small quantities of preserves can often be made while I am cooking the dinner at night. I take all the short cuts and it doesn't take long to peel a kilo of peaches or mangoes or onions. I sometimes prepare the fruit or vegetables one night and cook them the next.

I love having freshly made preserves. Home-made stuff has twice the flavour of commercial products, they need no preservatives and are so yummy. If you make good use of your freezer, microwave and food processor it is surprising what your own skill can provide for the pantry and table with a small outlay in money and time. You don't even need an especially well-equipped kitchen. The microwave and food processor make it quicker, but you can manage quite well without them.

Equipment you will need

- Kitchen scales
- Sharp knives – some small for peeling, some large for chopping.
- High-sided saucepan – this is essential to prevent boil-overs while you answer the phone or wipe the baby's nose.
- Slotted spoon
- Wooden spoons
- Sieve or Mouli-mill
- Potato/vegetable peeler
- Large chopping board

I also make good use of these items:

- Potato masher
- Blender and/or food processor
- Funnel – for filling sauce bottles
- Small jug with a spout – for filling jars
- Marmalade shredder – available at good kitchen shops and a great help at marmalade time.
- Fireproof mat

A word on pans

A heavy-bottomed pan helps to prevent sticking during cooking. Stainless steel or aluminium pans are most versatile. Jam cooks well in copper but any mixture in which vinegar is used will cause a corrosive reaction between the acid and the copper and give the preserves an unpleasant taste. So you will need an aluminium pan or stainless steel pan for pickles, relishes, chutneys or sauces.

Selecting and preparing the fruit

Generally the fruit and vegetables should be sound and ripe, but if your neighbour hands you a bucket of apricots or chokos over the fence because she has too many and they are getting too ripe to use, don't despair. They are still quite usable. Just cut out the over-ripe bits, throw away the rotten ones, wash them well and proceed.

Pectin is a starchy substance found in the cell walls of most fruit. When combined with heat and sugar this is what causes the preserves to set. Very ripe fruit contains less pectin and you may need to add more acid, such as lemon juice, tartaric acid or commercial pectin, which you can sometimes buy in supermarkets and is usually available in health food stores.

Some fruits need peeling, some are cut up small, and some used whole. For jam the fruit is usually cut up, for preserves it is usually left whole or in big pieces. For pickles the vegetables are chunky and for chutneys and relishes they are cut up.

Everything must be carefully washed. Soil residues can cause mould, and with so many fruits and vegetables being frequently sprayed when grown commercially it is very important to wash any residue from the skins.

Sugar and vinegar are the main preserving agents used for jam and pickle making and, provided the preserves are cooked enough, they should keep indefinitely.

What to put them in

Recycling is a popular catchword these days and no jar is ever thrown out in my house. As they are emptied I wash them and soak off the labels. It's easier to soak the labels off one or two jars at a time than wait until you want to use them and have to soak a whole sink full or, horror of horrors, leave them on. There's something a bit off-putting about marmalade in a jar labelled 'peanut butter'. I put them through the full cycle in the dishwasher and put them away till needed.

It is most important when preparing jars for any sort of preserves that they be scrupulously clean and dry. There are several ways of doing this:

Wash them in hot water and detergent.

Rinse carefully and dry them in an oven at 100–120°C with the door propped open.

Put them through the full dishwasher cycle and just before using dry them again in the microwave for 5–6 minutes on high.

Soak them in Milton solution as you would soak babies' bottles and dry in the microwave or oven.

Metal lids cannot be microwaved and should be soaked in Milton solution or sodium metabisulphite and carefully dried. This is available from chemists and can also be used as a preservative for preventing mould in dried fruit.

Covering and labelling

I save jars with screw-top lids, keeping the plastic or plastic-lined lids for pickles, chutneys, relishes or anything preserved in vinegar. The vinegar in the mixture causes corrosion of the metal lids. Wax or waxed paper can be placed between the mixture and metal lid but is not as satisfactory as a plastic lid.

If you don't have enough plastic lids buy a packet of jam seals from the supermarket. These contain circles of cellophane and rubber bands. Dip the cellophane circles in vinegar and place over jar. Tighten with rubber band. As the vinegar dries the cellophane will stretch tightly and seal. Metal lids can be placed over these or they can be left as they are. We live in the country and have mice come in from the bush. They don't take any time to demolish cellophane lids to get to the contents so I always use a lid as well.

You can also use plain brown paper soaked in vinegar and stuck down onto the jar. This looks very attractive but the mice can get into that too.

Label jars and bottles with the name of the contents and date. There are very nice labels available from gift shops and it is possible, if you like, to have an individual one printed with something like 'From the kitchen of . . .'. I use stick-on labels from the newsagent.

You can make jams, jellies, pickles and preserves from almost any edible fruit or vegetable. If you read the recipes in this book you will see that the same techniques prevail throughout. Once you gain confidence and expertise you can create your own combinations. If you have a bucket of kiwi fruit, plums, nectarines, or mangoes you can do what I do and adapt recipes to suit whatever fruit or vegetable you have in abundance.

If you live in Victoria or New South Wales you will quite likely have a hedge of feijoas, if not in your own garden then somewhere nearby. In Queensland you might have a huge mango tree in your yard, or chokos growing all over your back fence. In Tasmania you might live up the road from a berry farm. Anywhere in Australia you could have a supply of fruit that falls to the ground and rots away every year. It is a shame to see it go to waste, so recycle it! Anyone can do it. It is really very easy.

There are a few traps of course. Some vegetables and fruit have more pectin than others and set easily. Some need slow cooking to bring out the flavour, some need to be cooked fast, but once you become familiar with the techniques the possibilities are unlimited. You can combine the fruit you have available in mixtures no-one has tried yet. I wonder who first thought of tomato and rhubarb jam? This seems an unlikely combination at first, but it is terrific.

Browse through these pages on winter nights and when summer comes with all its bounty you will be ready to give it a go.

SHELLING PEAS
Sitting at the kitchen table
shelling peas
into a white china bowl
on yellow laminex
casting pods onto spread newspaper
she sits, hand-arm rhythm
splitting open full pods
running a finger along
rows of hard green marbles
dropping into the bowl
in rows like milk
from a cow's teat
steaming into a bucket
at sunrise.

Susan Perry, July 1992

CHAPTER TWO

*J*ams

No mean woman can cook well, for it calls for a light head,
a generous spirit, and a large heart.
(Paul Gauguin)

Sweet treats are frowned on by many in this health-conscious age, but I can't think of a nicer way to start the day than with wholemeal toast and home-made strawberry jam or blackberry jelly or kiwi fruit conserve. On Sunday mornings you can really indulge with fresh croissants or bagels with home-made quince jam or apple butter, then make up for it by having a salad for lunch.

APRICOTS

Apricots are one of the best summer fruits. They make wonderful jams and chutneys, great pies and cakes, and are also good for drying. The sight of ripe fruit dropping around the tree in suburban and country backyards is a common one in late January. It always makes me think of all the lovely things that could be made out of all that fruit.

My husband's cousin Elma lives in South Australia where they grow the best apricots. The soil and sun seem just right for them there. Elma's apricot jam is thick and spreads easily. She cuts the apricots up and cooks them first in the microwave. She does not use any water. Here is her recipe.

Apricot Jam
2 kg apricots, stoned and chopped
1 $^1/_2$ kg sugar
2 lemons cut in half

Put apricots and lemon halves in a microwave-proof bowl and cook on high for 15 minutes or until the fruit is soft. Stir frequently. Remove lemons and discard. Transfer the fruit to the pan, add sugar and stir until sugar is dissolved. Boil rapidly until setting test is reached. Apricot jam does not set as stiff as some other jams. Bottle while still hot.

Apricot Conserve
1 kg apricots
1 kg sugar
1 cup water
juice of 1 large lemon
6–8 apricot kernels

Make a syrup of the water and sugar by dissolving sugar over low heat, stirring constantly, then bring to the boil and let it boil for 4-5 minutes. Do not stir after the sugar has dissolved. Add halved apricots with stones removed, and lemon juice. Bring to a brisk boil and cook until setting test is reached. Add the kernels when the jam is almost cooked. Cool slightly. Bottle and seal.

Apricot Jam in the Microwave
500 g apricots
juice of 2 lemons
500 g sugar

Cut up apricots, add lemon juice and cook on high for 5 minutes. Mash with a potato masher two or three times. Add sugar and microwave on high for 3 minutes or until the sugar is dissolved, stirring two or three times. Microwave on high for 12 minutes or until setting point is reached. Stir several times. Bottle and seal.

Dried Apricots

When you are really tired of winter and long for the taste and smell of summer, treat yourself to a couple of packets of dried apricots (one for making jam and one for nibbling while you make it) and make up a batch of this jam. It will be gone in a couple of days and you'll have to make another batch.

Dried Apricot Jam

250 g dried apricots
1 kg sugar
1 L water x 2

Boil the first litre of water and pour over the apricots while hot. Leave to soak overnight. Strain off the excess juice. Put the apricots in a pan with the second litre of water and simmer gently until the apricots are tender. Add the sugar and stir until it is dissolved. Boil till setting test is reached. Bottle and seal.

Dried Apricot and Pumpkin Jam

My grandmother's apricot jam was much prized in our family and there always seemed to be an endless supply of it. When she got too old to be bothered making jam she passed the secret on to my mother who did the same for me. The famous apricot jam was made with dried apricots and pumpkin. It's a great recipe and you certainly can't taste the pumpkin.

225 g dried apricots, cut into pieces
700 mL water
450 g good bright-yellow pumpkin
8 tablespoons lemon juice
1 kg sugar

Soak the dried apricots overnight in 500 mL of water. The next day, peel the pumpkin into small chunks and cook gently in the rest of the water and lemon juice. Pour in the soaked apricots and water and cook for a further 10 minutes. Add the sugar and bring to the boil again, stirring until sugar is dissolved. Bottle and seal.

Dried Apricot and Carrot Jam

250 g dried apricots, cut into strips
600 mL water
500 g carrots
100 mL lemon juice
1 $^1/_2$ kg sugar

Soak the apricots in water overnight. Wash and peel the carrots and put them through a grater or blender. Place all ingredients in a pan and bring to the boil, stirring constantly until the sugar is dissolved.

Boil until setting point is reached, stirring frequently to prevent sticking. Bottle and seal.

BANANAS

Banana Jam

550 g ripe peeled bananas
350 g sugar
juice of 1 lemon
juice of 3 sweet oranges

Slice the bananas and combine with juices and sugar. Boil slowly until the mixture thickens and becomes a rich colour. Bottle and seal. This banana jam has extra flavour if brown sugar is used. It makes a beautiful first layer for a fruit flan.

Banana and Apple Jam

500 g ripe bananas
2 large cooking apples
grated rind and juice of 2 lemons
500 g sugar
100 mL water

Peel and core the apples and simmer in the water and lemon rind until soft. Add the sliced bananas, lemon juice and sugar. Stir until sugar is dissolved. Boil rapidly until setting point is reached. Bottle and seal.

BERRIES

Blackberries

Blackberries are probably the most delicious fruit in the world borne by a noxious weed. Because they are a noxious weed, and most councils make some attempt to keep them controlled, it is not a good idea to pick them from the side of the road. If they have not been sprayed in the current year they could still have residues from a previous attempt to knock them out. Look for a spot to pick them on a creek bank or up a quiet country lane where they are much less likely to have been sprayed.

You can often buy blackberries in punnets but they are large hybrid ones and do not have the same flavour as the 'picked-up-the-country-lane' variety. Wild blackberries are not generally as juicy as cultivated ones. They are usually smaller and harder and will require longer cooking to extract the pectin. They can be combined with apple or rhubarb in the same way as other berries but may need more cooking than the apple and rhubarb. Adding a few unripe blackberries makes the jam set better. They can be removed before bottling.

Blackberry Jam

500 g blackberries
400 g sugar

Mash blackberries in a pan to bring out the juice, then heat gently to boiling point. Boil for 5 minutes. Add sugar, stir until sugar is dissolved, then boil briskly for another 5 minutes or until setting test is reached. If the blackberries are very ripe you may need to add lemon juice.

Blackberry Jam in the Microwave

500 g blackberries
juice of 2 lemons
500 g sugar

Put the blackberries and lemon juice in a microwave-safe bowl and microwave for 5 minutes to soften the blackberries. Mash with a potato masher once or twice. When the berries are soft stir in the sugar and microwave for 2 minutes or until the sugar is dissolved. Microwave on high until setting point is reached. Stir once or twice. Bottle and seal.

Tom's Blackcurrant Jam

I bribe my grandson Tom to pick the blackcurrants for me by letting him make the jam and sharing the result.

quantity of blackcurrants.

water

sugar

Measure the blackcurrants by cup. For every cup of blackcurrants add 1 scant cup of water. Simmer the fruit and water until the fruit is soft and mushy. Add 1 cup of sugar for every cup of blackcurrants (measured dry before adding water). Stir carefully until the sugar is all dissolved then boil briskly without stirring until a little jam will set on a saucer placed in the freezer for a few minutes. Remove the jam from the heat, allow to stand for a few minutes, then pour carefully into sterilised jars and seal. This jam should require only about 10 minutes boiling after the sugar is added. It is a truly magnificent jam with a unique flavour.

Blackcurrant and Rhubarb Jam

770 g rhubarb, finely sliced, strings removed

300 mL water

700 g blackcurrants

another 600 mL water

2 kg sugar

Cook the rhubarb to a pulp with 300 mL of water. Add the blackcurrants, the 600 mL of water and the sugar. Stir well until the sugar is dissolved, then boil rapidly till setting point is reached. Bottle and seal.

This recipe works just as well with red currants.

Blueberry Jam

500 g blueberries (2 punnets)

500 g sugar

juice and grated rind of 3 lemons

200 mL water

Put blueberries, water, lemon juice and rind in a saucepan. Simmer until berries are soft. Add sugar, stirring till it is dissolved. Boil briskly until setting point is reached. Bottle and seal.

Gooseberries
Gooseberries can be quite hard to get in Australia now. A few years ago a mildew known as American gooseberry mildew wiped out most of the gooseberries in the southern states. If yours were lucky enough to survive and you still have some fruit, here are some tasty jams to make.

Gooseberry Jam
1 kg gooseberries
1.2 L of water
juice of 3 lemons
sugar
Boil the gooseberries in the water with the lemon juice until they turn pink. Measure the fruit mixture and for every cup add 1 cup of sugar. Boil rapidly until thick and pulpy and setting point is reached. Bottle and seal.

Gooseberry and Apple Jam
700 g gooseberries
900 g cooking apples
1.6 kg sugar
knob of butter
Wash, top and tail gooseberries. Peel, core and chop apples. Put them both in a pan with 300 mL of water and boil until the fruit is soft and pulpy and the gooseberries turn pink. Add the sugar and stir until it is dissolved. Add the knob of butter. Boil until setting point is reached. Bottle and seal.

Gooseberry and Strawberry Jam
700 g strawberries
130 mL water
700 g gooseberries, washed and stems removed
1.4 kg sugar
Put the gooseberries and water in a pan and simmer until tender. Add sugar

and strawberries. Stir gently till sugar is dissolved then boil rapidly until setting point is reached. Bottle and seal.

Mixed Berry Jam

3 cups mixed berries
2 $\frac{1}{2}$ cups sugar
juice of 1 large lemon

Cook blackberries with a minimum amount of water until soft. Add the other berries, lemon juice and sugar. Stir until sugar is dissolved. Boil briskly until setting test is reached. Skim, bottle and seal.

Mulberries

Mulberries are part of summer to me. My husband's mother had an enormous tree in her backyard in Mildura and our children would make a beeline for it whenever we visited – with disastrous results for their clothes and white sandals. The mulberry is a hardy tree which grows well in the hotter and drier parts of Australia but will also grow in cooler areas.

Mulberry Jam

1 kg mulberries
100 mL water
800 g sugar
juice of 2 lemons

Put the mulberries, water and lemon juice in a pan and simmer until the berries are soft and mushy. Add the sugar and stir until it is dissolved. Boil rapidly until setting point is reached. Bottle and seal.

Raspberries

Raspberry jam is one of the most luxurious of jams. We live in an area where they are grown commercially, so I can always get them in jam quantities for a reasonable price. If you have to pay bags of money for a punnet of raspberries where you live you can still get that raspberry flavour by combining them with a cheaper fruit like plums, apples or rhubarb. It's not quite as good as straight raspberry but it comes close. It is an easy jam to make and sets best if cooked in small quantities. This also preserves the fresh raspberry taste.

Raspberry Jam
500 g raspberries (2 punnets)
500 g sugar
Put raspberries in the pan and mash slightly with a potato masher or wooden spoon until enough juice is extracted to prevent the fruit sticking to the bottom of the pan. Bring to the boil and boil rapidly, stirring frequently. Add the sugar to the boiling pulp. Stir until the sugar is dissolved and the mixture boils again, then boil hard for 4 minutes or until setting point is reached. Allow the mixture to cool a little, then bottle and seal.

Raspberry Jam in the Microwave
500 g raspberries (2 punnets)
juice of two lemons
500 g sugar
Put the raspberries, sugar and lemon juice in a microwave-safe bowl and microwave on high for 5 minutes or until the sugar is dissolved. Stir frequently. When the sugar is dissolved microwave the mixture on high for another 12–14 minutes or until setting point is reached. Stir every 5 minutes. Bottle and seal.

Frozen raspberries can be used but thaw them out first.

Raspberry and Rhubarb Jam
2 kg rhubarb, skinned and finely sliced
1.2 kg sugar
1 kg raspberries (4 punnets)
Place the rhubarb in a plastic or crockery bowl. Sprinkle with sugar and leave overnight. In the morning, add the raspberries. Put all into a pan and bring to the boil, stirring until sugar is dissolved. Boil rapidly until setting point is reached. Bottle and seal.

Five-minute Strawberry Jam
1 kg strawberries (4 punnets)
1 ^{1}/$_2$ kg sugar
1 heaped teaspoon tartaric acid
Hull the strawberries and place the fruit and sugar in pan. Stir until boiling

and boil hard for 3 minutes. Add the tartaric acid and boil for another 5 minutes without stirring. Allow the mixture to become almost cold before bottling so that the fruit does not rise to the top in the syrup. Cover and seal.

Strawberry Jam in the Microwave

500 g strawberries (2 punnets)
$^1/_4$ cup lemon juice
2 cups sugar

Wash and hull the strawberries. Place them with the lemon juice in a microwave-safe bowl and microwave on high for 4 minutes or until strawberries are soft. Stir in the sugar and cook on high for another 20 minutes or until the jam gels in a saucer. Stand for 5 minutes before pouring into hot jars. Seal.

Strawberry and Apple Jam

Strawberries and raspberries, indeed any berries, can be very satisfactorily combined with apples or rhubarb to make jams with a bit more bulk while using less berries. Use about the same quantities of each fruit, but cook the rhubarb or apple a little first.

250 g apples, peeled, cored and chopped
$^1/_4$ cup water
250 g strawberries (1 punnet)
1 $^1/_2$ cups sugar
juice of 1 large lemon

Simmer the apples in water until soft. Add the strawberries and cook until blended and pulpy. Add the sugar and lemon juice and stir until the sugar is dissolved. Boil briskly until setting test is reached. Stand for 5 minutes then bottle and seal.

FEIJOAS

Suburban streets in Melbourne and Sydney abound in feijoa hedges. Most of the fruit falls on the ground. Here are two different ways to use some of them.

Your pretty green feijoas will turn brown when cooked and the jam is very sweet. It is a very good base for fruit flans. The sweet feijoa jam counteracts the acidity of the fresh fruit. I sometimes use it instead of custard for the first layer. I also use it diluted with water and brandy for a glaze.

Feijoa Jam
1 kg feijoas
100 mL water
800 g sugar
juice and grated rind of 2 lemons
Put the water in the bottom of the pan and add the sliced, washed feijoas, sugar, lemon juice and rind. Stir until the sugar is dissolved. Boil until setting point is reached. Bottle and seal.

Feijoa and Ginger Jam
1.8 kg feijoas, washed and chopped
120 g crystallised ginger, sliced finely
400 mL water
rind and juice of 2 lemons
1.8 kg sugar
Cook feijoas in water until the skins are soft. Add the rest of the ingredients. Bring to the boil stirring until the sugar is dissolved. Boil rapidly until setting point is reached. Bottle and seal.

FIGS

Figs are such a beautiful autumn fruit. They make wonderful jam and mouth-watering preserves. They are also easy to dry in the sun or in the oven. They freeze well enough for puddings and desserts but I have found jam made from frozen figs does not keep as well. They also combine well with apples and the jam is not as seedy.

Fig jam is simplicity itself. If you prefer a conserve-type jam just top and tail the figs, split them down the centre, and proceed as for fig jam. You will get a good chunky preserve.

FIGS

Figs are old
each tree looks it too
before people spoke
our languages
they ate figs
and no doubt
found them good
brown or purple
the skin is queer
striped furry sandpaper
and inside
the rent flesh lies
pink gorgeous wet
it doesn't throbb
but it might
and the scent
a mixture
of honey
earth rain
and something green.

the white sap
from the stem
turns milk sour
and that you see
is how Adam and Eve
made junket

they used a leaf
as a bowl
and technology was born
can't you see it
rising like Venus
from the cream
stretching its beautiful dangerous arms.

Kate Llewellyn.

Fig Jam

500 g fresh figs
400 g sugar
juice and grated rind of 2 lemons

Wash and slice the figs finely. Cover them with sugar and leave overnight in a plastic or ceramic bowl. The next day add the lemon juice and rind. Put the mixture in a pan and boil until setting point is reached. Bottle and seal.

Fig and Ginger Jam

500 g fresh figs
400 g sugar
100 g sliced or chopped crystallised ginger
juice and grated rind of 2 lemons

Slice the figs finely. Cover them with sugar and leave overnight in a plastic or ceramic bowl. The next morning add the ginger and lemon juice and rind. Boil until setting point is reached. Bottle and seal.

Dried Fig Jam

450 g dried figs
300 g sugar
juice and grated rind of 1 lemon

Soak the figs overnight in enough water to cover them. Strain the water into a pan. Chop the figs and add to the water. Simmer until tender. Add the sugar, lemon juice and rind and stir until the sugar is dissolved. Boil until setting point is reached. Bottle and seal. Dried fig and ginger jam can be made the same way by adding crystallised ginger to this recipe.

Kate Llewellyn's Mother's Fig Jam

Kate Llewellyn's mother is 90 years old and still makes magical fig jam.

$2 \frac{3}{4}$ kg figs
$2 \frac{3}{4}$ kg sugar
$\frac{1}{2}$ L water

Boil the chopped figs, sugar and water well for 1 hour. Add 2 tablespoons of vinegar and 1 cup of blanched almonds at the end of cooking. Bottle and seal. This jam turns to honey.

KIWI FRUIT

Kiwi Fruit and Citrus Jam
1 $^1/_2$ kg kiwi fruit, peeled and chopped
2 large oranges
3 lemons
700 g sugar

Peel the oranges and lemons with a sharp knife or vegetable peeler making sure to avoid any of the white pith. Cut the peeled skin into fine shreds with a sharp knife or a pair of kitchen scissors. Place the peel in a pan with the chopped and peeled kiwi fruit and the juice of the oranges and lemons. Cook gently until the rinds and kiwi fruit are tender. Add the sugar, stirring until it is dissolved. Boil briskly until setting point is reached. Bottle and seal.

Quick Kiwi Fruit Jam
Kiwi fruit will lose its colour if water is used. This method sets well and is a lovely light green colour.
1 kg kiwi fruit peeled
1 kg sugar

Slice up the kiwi fruit and put it in a ceramic or plastic bowl in layers with the sugar. Leave to stand overnight, pressing down frequently to extract the juice. The next morning put the fruit and sugar in a pan and bring to the boil, stirring until the sugar is dissolved. Boil rapidly for 5 minutes. Allow to cool slightly. Bottle and seal.

MANGOES

I am a passionate lover of mangoes. When I lived in Vanuatu we would buy a whole coconut basket full of them for almost nothing at our local Saturday market.

My husband is not a mango lover. He hasn't liked them since a fruit bat dropped one on the tin roof of our house the first night we spent in the tropics. He was convinced it was either artillery fire or an earthquake. I don't see why he should hold it against the mango, but then he doesn't like fruit bats much either.

No-one has yet found a way to keep mangoes over the winter so, if you need a mango fix on a cold wintry day, put some of this jam away for your breakfast toast or croissant.

Mango Jam

1 kg peeled and diced mango flesh
100 mL water
1 kg sugar
juice of 2 lemons

Place the mangoes, water and lemon juice in a pan and bring to the boil. Mash the mango flesh a little with a potato masher as it cooks. When the mangoes are soft and well mixed add the sugar. Stir until the sugar is dissolved, then boil briskly until the setting point is reached. It should take only about 10 minutes of boiling, depending on the ripeness of the mangoes.

Old-fashioned Mango Jam

This is an old recipe from the Pacific Islands.

Take nicely coloured but quite firm mangoes, cut the flesh from the seed and dice. Cut 4 heaped breakfast-cupfuls of mango and put it on to boil with 2 cupfuls of water. Boil gently for 15 minutes. Add 4 level cupfuls of sugar and boil briskly for 20–30 minutes.

That is all the recipe says. In those days one was expected to know the rest about mashing the mangoes as they cook and not stirring after the sugar is added and putting the jam into sterilised jars and so on.

MELONS

I haven't seen a jam melon for years. My mother always asked my father to bring one home from the market when they were in season. Jam melons are the best for all melon recipes but honeydew melons are a good substitute and need a little less sugar. Take out about half a cup of sugar from these recipes if you are using honeydew melon.

Melon, Lemon and Ginger Jam

1 kg of peeled, seeded and chopped melon
1 kg sugar
grated rind and juice of 1 lemon
250 g preserved ginger

Place the chopped melon in a pan with the lemon rind and juice, ginger and sugar and let the mixture stand overnight. The next day boil all the ingredients together gently until the melon is clear and the setting point is reached. Bottle and seal. Long, slow cooking is best for melon jam.

This jam was my father's favourite.

Melon and Passionfruit Jam

1 kg melon, peeled, seeded and chopped into small dice
1 kg sugar
6-8 passionfruit

Place the melon and sugar in a pan and let it stand overnight. The next day boil this mixture gently until setting point is almost reached. Add the passionfruit for the final 5 minutes of cooking. It can take over an hour for these melon jams to set, so give it time. The melon can be mashed with a potato masher while cooking to give the jam a more even consistency. Bottle and seal.

PAWPAWS

Pawpaw Jam

2 cups diced pawpaw
2 cups sugar
$^1/_2$ cup fresh lime juice (or lemon if limes are not available)

Boil briskly, stirring only until sugar is dissolved. Bottle and seal when set.

This is a very easy recipe and a good substitute for apricot jam. Soak a few dried apricots in lime juice and substitute them for some of the pawpaw and it tastes like the real thing. Apricot jam is greatly prized in the tropics just as mango or pawpaw jam is a treat in cold southern Victoria.

Pawpaw and Ginger Jam
750 g firm pawpaw, skinned and seeded
100 g preserved ginger
$^1/_2$ cup lemon juice
500 g sugar
Put the pawpaw and lemon juice in a pan. Simmer until tender. Add the sugar, stirring until it is dissolved. Add the ginger and boil rapidly until setting test is reached. Bottle and seal.

PEACHES

Yellow peaches make the best looking peach jam and preserves. Their firmer flesh stays intact better than other varieties. White peaches are quite suitable for jam and preserves but the colour is rather murky. Keep them for eating fresh.

Peach Jam
1 kg yellow peaches
1 cup water
750 g sugar
juice of 2 large lemons
Stone, peel and slice the peaches. Cook in the water until the fruit is soft. Add the sugar and lemon juice and stir until the sugar is dissolved. Boil briskly until setting point is reached. Bottle and seal.

Peach (or Nectarine) and Pineapple Jam
1 medium pineapple
500 g peaches or nectarines
1 tablespoon grated orange rind
1 tablespoon grated lemon rind
juice of 1 oragne and 1 lemon
6 cups sugar
Wash and cut up the fruit, removing stones and skin. Boil the fruit with the sugar, rinds and juices, stirring only until the sugar is dissolved. Keep boiling until setting point is reached. Bottle and seal.

PEARS

Pear and Walnut Jam

1 kg ripe pears
1 orange
1 kg sugar
100 mL water
125 g chopped walnuts

Peel and slice the pears and remove the core. Cut up the orange finely, leaving the skin on. Mash the pears slightly with a potato masher. Put the pears, water, orange and sugar into a pan and boil gently until the pears are turning pink and the mixture is thick. Approximately 10 minutes before setting point is reached, add the chopped walnuts. Cook until setting point is reached. Bottle and seal.

This is a crunchy jam, delicious on toast.

Pear and Ginger Jam

1 kg firm pears
juice and rind of 1 lemon
750 g sugar
200 g sugar

Peel and cut up the pears. Cover them with sugar and the lemon juice and grated rind of lemon and leave to stand overnight. The next day cut up the ginger as finely as you like. Some people like the flavour of the ginger but not the texture. Put the pears, ginger, lemon juice, rind and sugar in a pan. If there is not much liquid you may have to add a little water, just enough to prevent sticking. Boil all ingredients together until setting point is reached. Bottle and seal.

PINEAPPLES

Pineapple Jam (today's version)
1 fresh pineapple
sugar
juice of 2 lemons

Peel the pineapple and weigh it. Grate or vitamise it in the food processor, including the hard, core pieces. Stand it in a non-metallic bowl overnight with the lemon juice and an equal amount of sugar. The next day boil briskly until setting point is reached. Bottle and seal.

Pineapple Jam (yesterday's version)
9 pineapples
9 lemons
5 ^{3}/4 kg sugar

Remove peel from the pines, slice and cut into small squares or grate. Cover with sugar and allow to stand for 24 hours. Put in a pan, add strained juice and grated lemon rind. Boil till it will set. Put in jars and when cool tie down securely and keep in a dry place.

I wonder how many jars that recipe will make!

PLUMS

Plums are the summer fruit we always have. Even if every other crop in the garden fails there are always plenty of plums. I know older people who will never let plum jam pass their lips these days. They say it was all they had in the 1930s depression.

I can't say I am mad about plain old plum jam either – having eaten my share of it at school on steamed puddings and jam roly poly. However, it is a good jam to learn on as it sets easily, and combined with other fruits can be a gastronomic *tour de force*.

Plum Jam

1 kg plums
750 g sugar
1 cup water

Wash the fruit and, if you are using large red or yellow plums, remove the stones. If you are using cherry plums or damson plums leave the stones in. Boil the cup of water and half the sugar for 5 minutes, stirring until the sugar is dissolved. Add the fruit and bring the mixture slowly to the boil. Boil until the fruit is soft and pulpy, then remove the stones with a slotted spoon. Add the rest of the sugar, stir until boiling well and cook until setting point is reached. Cool slightly, bottle and seal.

Plum and Elderberry Jam

Elderberries are light in weight and it takes quite a few to make up 200 g. I find that even a cup of elderberries added to any plum mixture gives a piquant spicy flavour to plain old plum jam. If more than a cup of elderberries is added the same weight in plums should be removed. Use the same quantities and method as plain old plum.

TOMATOES

Tomato Jam

1 ^{1}/$_2$ kg tomatoes, skinned and sliced
500 g apples, peeled and chopped
finely grated rind and juice of 2 lemons
1 ^{1}/$_4$ kg sugar

Put the tomatoes, apples, lemon juice and rind in a pan and simmer until the apples and tomatoes are tender and partially blended. Add the sugar, stirring until it is dissolved. Boil until setting point is reached. Bottle and seal.

Tomato and Rhubarb Jam

1 kg ripe tomatoes
300 g rhubarb
1 tablespoon grated lemon rind

$^1/_2$ cup lemon juice

1 kg sugar

Skin and slice the tomatoes. Skin and cube the rhubarb. Put the tomatoes, rhubarb, lemon juice and rind in a pan and bring to the boil. Simmer for half an hour, stirring to prevent sticking. Add the sugar to the mixture, stirring until it is completely dissolved. Bring to the boil and boil rapidly until setting point is reached. Bottle and seal.

OTHER FRUIT

Cherry Jam

To me it always seems a crime to eat cherries any way but fresh, but if you should happen to have a surfeit and are a fan of cherry jam here is a recipe.

600 g cherries

juice of 2 large lemons

400 g sugar

Simmer cherries in lemon juice, and a little extra water to prevent sticking, until the fruit is soft and the stones rise to the top. Remove the stones with a slotted spoon. Add the sugar, stirring until it is dissolved, then boil rapidly until setting point is reached. To improve the flavour, add a few drops of almond essence before the jam is removed from the heat. Stand for a few minutes. Stir well so that the cherries don't rise to the top. Bottle and seal.

Choko Jam

12 chokos

juice of 6 lemons

100 g finely chopped crystallised ginger

half a cup of sugar to each cup of cut-up chokos

Peel and cut up the chokos. Add the lemon juice and stand overnight. In the morning pour off excess juice and cook fruit with 2 cups of water until tender. Measure the pulp and allow half a cup of sugar for every cup of pulp. Add the ginger and boil briskly until setting test is reached. Bottle and seal.

Guavas

Guavas are a lot like chokos. If you have them, you have millions. They have a lot of seeds which are difficult to remove. It is not absolutely necessary to remove them, but the jam is better without the seeds.

Guava Jam

1 kg guavas
1 kg sugar
juice and grated rind of 2 lemons
200 mL water

It is necessary to peel the guavas and put the pulp through a Mouli-mill or stir it all through a sieve to remove the seeds. When this is done combine the guava pulp with the sugar and lemon juice and rind. Boil the mixture until it is thick. Setting test may not be reached with this jam and it will be more like a sauce or a honey. It is very good on ice-cream.

Loquat Jam

This is a good way to use all those thousands of loquats that fall off the tree in late spring.

1 kg loquats
200 mL water
juice and rind of 2 lemons

Squeeze the seeds out of the loquats but leave the skin on. (This can be a messy operation.) Put the fruit in the pan with the water and simmer until the fruit is soft. Put this through a blender or Mouli-mill. Measure the fruit back into the pan by cup and for very cup of pulp add three-quarters of a cup of sugar. Add the lemon rind and juice and bring to the boil, stirring constantly until the sugar is dissolved. Boil rapidly until setting point is reached. Bottle and seal.

Nectarines

Nectarines are such a good late summer fruit. Our family often ate them for breakfast, freshly cut up with a little sugar and cream, or stewed with cream or ice-cream after the evening meal. As with many fruits and vegetables those grown in the home orchard often seem to have the best flavour. If you have an old tree that bears well you will probably eat most of them fresh as they are so delicious. But if you have more than you can use, this jam is very refreshing and keeps well.

Nectarine Jam

1 ^{1}/$_2$ kg nectarines
1 tablespoon grated orange rind
1 tablespoon grated lemon rind
juice of 1 orange and 1 lemon
6 cups of sugar

Wash the fruit, remove the stones and cut up. Boil the fruit with the sugar, rinds and juices, stirring only until sugar is dissolved. Boil until setting point is reached. Bottle and seal immediately.

Persimmons

There is no tree quite as beautiful as a persimmon in autumn and winter. The leaves are wondrously coloured and when they eventually fall, the golden balls of the fruit hang on the bare branches like glowing lanterns. Unripe persimmons are sour, mouth-puckering fruit but when they are soft and custardy inside they are food for the gods. You need to leave them on the tree as long as possible to get the beautiful colour. If you can bring yourself to pick them before the blackbirds move in you can finish ripening them inside a plastic bag containing a ripe apple. If you have a tree full here is a recipe for you.

Persimmon Jam

4 really ripe persimmons (add an extra one if they are small)
500 g sugar
100 g grated fresh pineapple
1 tablespoon lemon or lime juice
grated peel of lemon or lime

Peel the persimmons by cutting diagonally across the top and peeling back the skin. Scoop out the persimmon pulp and combine with the sugar. Mash with a potato masher to combine the fruit and sugar well. Cook gently for 10 minutes, stirring constantly. Just bring the mixture to the boil, then remove it from the heat and add the pineapple, lemon juice and rind. Cook for a further 5 minutes. Bottle and seal.

Quandongs

Quandongs are small, tart, bright red fruits that are native to Australia. They are reputed to have a very high vitamin C content. The trees are related to sandalwood and appear to be semi-parasitic. They are found in the wild near other trees. Quandongs grow in the drier parts of inland Australia. Experiments and field trials are being conducted to try and grow them commercially. There is one quandong farm on the Eyre Peninsula in South Australia. We hope they will be available in markets before too long.

Under the thin red skin they have a layer of yellow flesh around large kernels. The kernels are edible and look like Chinese checkers. They can also be used for necklaces.

We had a tree growing by the house gate at our Mallee farm and looked forward to a special treat every spring. We also went on quandong foraging picnics to supplement the crop from our one tree and to get enough fruit to make a pie and maybe some jam as well. My husband claims he is not set up for the year unless he gets his annual quandong pie. The taste of the cooked fruit is quite unlike any other, although I have heard it described as a tarter and more fully-flavoured version of rhubarb.

Quandong Jam

$2\,^1/2$ cups washed and stoned quandongs (do not soak the fruit in water)
2 cups of sugar
squeeze of lemon juice
$^1/4$–$^1/2$ cup of water

Boil the fruit with the lemon juice for 20 minutes until tender, add the sugar and stir until it is dissolved. Simmer until the mixture turns a deep reddish colour with a few golden bubbles on top of the jam, then turn the heat down low and simmer until the mixture is slightly thickened. It should be a nice thick consistency. Bottle and seal.

Quince Jam
550 g quinces
500 g sugar
water

Core the quinces. Put them into a pan and just cover with water. Keep the seeds and cores, and tie them all in a small muslin bag. Put this in the water with the quinces. Simmer gently until the quinces are soft and turning pink. Add sugar, stir until dissolved. Boil rapidly until setting point is reached. Remove the bag of cores and seeds. Allow the jam to stand until it is almost cold before bottling to prevent the fruit rising in the syrup.

Rose Petal Jam

There is a lot written about rose petal preserves and jams. I have not had much success without using commercial pectin. Rose-hip jam had the same problem. By the time they reached setting point they had lost all their beauty and were a murky colour. Now I use commercial, powdered pectin and both jams are easy.

225 g red or pink rose petals (picked when fully open but not ready to drop;
   this is a lot of rose petals)
450 g sugar
juice of 2 lemons
commercial pectin for 250 g of fruit (according to directions on the packet)

Remove petals from the roses and cut off the white part at the base. Cut the petals in half. Put them into a ceramic bowl (not plastic as it absorbs the scent of the roses). Sprinkle with half the sugar and leave to stand overnight. Pour 1 L of water in the pan with the lemon juice and the rest of the sugar. Heat and stir until the sugar is dissolved. When the mixture is just simmering add the rose petals and simmer for half an hour. Add the commercial pectin and bring to quick boil for 5 minutes. Bottle and seal.

Tamarillo Jam
1 kg tamarillos
800 g sugar
200 mL water
grated rind and juice of 2 lemons

Peel and slice the tamarillos. (They peel easily after being placed in boiling water for a few minutes.) Place all ingredients in a pan and bring to the boil, stirring until the sugar is dissolved. Boil until setting point is reached. Bottle and seal.

MALLEE IN OCTOBER

When clear October suns unfold
mallee tips of red and gold,

children on their way to school
discover tadpoles in a pool,

iceplants sheathed in beaded glass,
spider orchids and shivery grass,

webs with globes of dew alight,
budgerigars on their first flight,

tottery lambs and stilty foal,
a papery slough that a snake shed whole,

and a bronzewing's nest of twigs so few
that both the sky and the eggs show through.

Flexmore Hudson

CHAPTER THREE

*J*ellies

While the pot boils, friendship blooms.
(A. B. Cheales)

JELLY MAKING

Jelly making is supposed to be a difficult and skilled operation best left to superior cooks. This is all a myth. Jelly making is a breeze. It is easier than jam making. No peeling or dicing is needed, just rough cutting up. It can be made in two separate operations on two separate days or nights if necessary, and for those of us who have only short periods of time available it is a very rewarding pastime. People love jars of home-made jellies, which look wonderful bottled in small jars. They are good for gifts if you cover the lid in a pretty cloth or paper and tie with a ribbon. And they simply dance off the stall at school fetes.

All this is provided you don't mind having a jelly bag hanging from an up-ended kitchen stool on your kitchen bench for days at a time.

Jelly is simply the strained extract of well-cooked fruit combined with an equal quantity of sugar till the 'gel' or setting test is reached. The fruit should not be too ripe. Here is where the abundance of apples and crab apples, no matter how small and miserable, can be used. Crab apples especially are rich in pectin (which makes the jelly set) and can be combined with all sorts of fruits and herbs to make marvellous jellies.

Millions of crab apples fall to the ground all over Australia every year, so make jelly and use them in a positive way. Any crab apples or apples are suitable. Here is what you do.

Using any quantity of fruit (small quantities of about 2 kg are easier to handle). Wash well to remove dust, spray residue and so on, and place in a pan. Small fruits like crab apples or plums can be left whole while large fruits like apples or quinces are best cut in half. No peeling or coring is required. Just cover them with water. Firmer fruits need a bit more water. Simmer until the fruit is soft but not mushy.

While the fruit is cooking prepare your straining set-up. This is where you will require the co-operation of the family. I up-end the kitchen stool and secure a piece of cheesecloth about 1 m square from each leg. You can use a small nail or drawing pin or tie the corners of the material to each stool leg. Place a large basin or pan under the suspended cheesecloth bag. (To fail to do this, as I once did, results in the loss of a lot of valuable fruit essence and makes an awful, sticky mess on the kitchen floor.)

I put my stool on the floor while I pour the cooked fruit and water into the jelly bag. If you are making a large quantity get someone to help you pour straight by holding the edges of the bag a bit apart. There is a risk of the hot mixture splashing up while you do this, so make sure the baby, cat or dog are not in the immediate area. Simply pour the fruit through the bag all at once and let it drip into the bowl underneath. This can and does take ages and I often leave it overnight, or for up to 24 hours, with no ill-effects. This is in the cool central highlands. I don't think I would leave it as long in the tropics, as the fruit might ferment. But it is quite all right to let it drip overnight and store the fruit essence in the fridge for the day if you only have time to cook in the evenings. Don't be tempted to help it along by stirring or squeezing the bag as this will only result in a cloudy jelly.

When the fruit is finished dripping, measure the extract by the cup and return it to the cooking pan adding one cup of sugar for every cup of extract. Heat gently, stirring until the sugar is dissolved before allowing to boil. Then boil briskly until setting test is reached. Bottle the jelly while it is still hot. Seal and label. I told you it was a breeze!

In case I have confused you in the preceding instructions, here it is again in six steps.

1   Wash fruit and cover with water.
2   Boil till soft but not mushy.
3   Pour through the jelly bag.
4   Add 1 cup of sugar for every cup of extract.
5   Stir till sugar is dissolved and boil till set.
6   Bottle and seal while hot.

The setting test is the same as for jam. It will set when a little bit of jelly placed on a saucer and put in the freezer for a few minutes wrinkles when the saucer is tilted. This is when you remove the mixture from the heat.

FRUIT JELLIES

Basic Apple Jelly
quantity of apples
water
sugar

Wash apples and cut in half, leaving the skins on and the cores in. Just cover with water. Simmer for an hour or so until the fruit is soft. Pour the mixture through a jelly bag. For every cup of extract add one cup of sugar. Stir until the sugar is dissolved then boil briskly until the setting test is reached. Bottle, seal and label.

Crab Apple Jelly
This is made in exactly the same way as apple or quince jelly. As in jam making the combinations are endless. Use half-and-half fruit, or roughly equal quantities of combinations. Here are some of my favourite combinations.

- Quince and apple jelly
- Plum and apple jelly
- Elderberry and apple jelly
- Gooseberry and apple jelly

- Rosehip and apple jelly
- Guava and apple jelly

For any of these combination recipes crab apples can be used instead of apples in exactly the same way. Here are a few other special jellies.

Japonica Jelly

For some peculiar reason japonicas are also known as chaenomeles but chaenomeles jelly sounds like an infectious disease. I shall stick to the old name of japonica. Japonicas are the nuggetty little quinces that form on the flowering japonica bushes in autumn. They make a clear amber jelly.

$2\,^{1}/_{2}$ kg japonica quinces

water to just cover

Simmer the fruit as for other jellies. Pour through a jelly bag and add 1 cup of sugar for every cup of extract. Boil briskly till set. Bottle and seal.

Quince Jelly

There are two methods of making quince jelly. One is the same as for apple jelly where exactly the same proportions and method are used. The other is even less complicated but takes longer. The bonus is that you have the delicious quinces left at the end of the cooking, which can be eaten as a dessert with cream or ice-cream.

Auntie Daph's Quince Jelly

2 kg quinces

2 kg sugar

10 cups of water

Wipe the quinces well, removing all the cottony fuzz on the skins. Do not cut them up but place them whole in the pan and pour over the water and sugar. Boil gently for about 4–5 hours until the jelly will set in a saucer. Remove the whole quinces carefully with a spoon and serve as a dessert. Bottle and seal the jelly.

Special Quince Jelly Preserve

Peel and slice a few of the smaller riper quinces into slices about 1 cm thick. Chop the rest of the quinces roughly, cover them with water and lay the quince slices on top. Simmer until the quince slices are tender and a lovely pink colour, then remove them whole with a slotted spoon. Simmer the rest of the quinces until they are soft and pour the mixture through a jelly bag. For each cup of extract add 1 cup of sugar and proceed as for other jellies, adding 2 cinnamon sticks to the mixture. When the setting test is reached remove the cinnamon sticks. Place the sliced quinces in the bottom of the jars and pour the jelly over the top. The quince slices must be covered by the jelly. Bottle, seal and label. This preserve looks very elegant.

QUINCES
the tree stood there
giving us green lamps
which we picked

I took them to you
and put them on a blue plate
you shook your head and smiled

there they sat
this curious fruit
that cut has the texture of wet chalk
and cooked
turns not like water to wine
but fruit to blood.

Excerpt from *Quinces* by Kate Llewellyn

Medlars

Medlars are an unusual fruit. The tree is frequently grown as an ornamental as it has lovely white flowers in spring and stunning autumn foliage. The fruits are edible and make good jelly and a piquant, richly flavoured butter. They are small, green and round with fringed, pointed calyx segments. They will not ripen on the tree. I pick them when they begin to go brown (I have to beat the possums to it!), and ripen them in the house. They are hard and green inside when picked but left for about three weeks will become soft and brown inside, ready for eating or cooking. Use only fully ripened medlars.

Medlar Jelly

quantity of medlars

Cut the medlars in half and place them in a pan. Cover with water in the usual way. For each 5 cups of pulp add 1 sliced lemon and 2 cinnamon sticks. Boil until the fruit is soft (about 20 minutes). Strain mixture through a jelly bag. Add 1 cup of sugar for each cup of extract. Boil briskly until setting point is reached. Bottle and seal. This jelly keeps well and improves with age.

Feijoa Jelly

1 kg feijoas
sugar
lemon juice

Peel the feijoas and cut them in half. Cover with water and simmer until the fruit is soft. Strain through a jelly bag. For each cup of extract add 1 cup of sugar and 1 tablespoon of strained lemon juice. Boil briskly until setting point is reached. Bottle, seal and label.

Feijoa and Guava Jelly

1 $\frac{1}{4}$ kg feijoas
500 g guavas
1 kg slightly under-ripe apples

Chop the fruit into quarters or eighths, leaving seeds in. Place in a pan and cover with water. Boil until soft but not too mushy. If the mixture becomes too mushy the jelly will be cloudy. Strain through a jelly bag overnight. Discard the contents of bag and measure the juice extracted. Allow 1 scant cup of sugar for each cup of juice. Bring to the boil, stirring only until the sugar is dissolved. Boil rapidly until setting test is reached. Bottle and seal.

Grape Jelly

6 cups black or green grapes
2 green apples

Remove the stems from grapes and place with cut up apples (skins and core included) in a pan. Cover with water. Simmer until fruit is tender. Pour through a jelly bag. Add 1 cup of sugar for each cup of water and the strained juice of 1 lemon. Boil briskly until setting point is reached.

Green grapes make a golden coloured jelly, black grapes a rich ruby red jelly.

Hawthorns

Whatever fruits we lack in the area where I live hawthorns are not one of them. Not many people realise that the fruits from the miles and miles of hawthorn hedges are great for jelly making. The birds will not appreciate your stealing from their winter food store, so leave plenty for them. But do try this tasty jelly.

Hawthorn Jelly

1 ^{1}/2 kg Hawthorn berries
juice of 3 lemons
sugar

Pick the berries when they are nice and red (after the first frost is a good time). Wash them well and put in a pan. Cover with water. Simmer over a low heat until berries are tender, mashing the fruit with the potato masher from time to time to extract the pectin. Strain through a jelly bag. Add 1 scant cup of sugar for each cup of liquid. Stir in the lemon juice and boil until setting point is reached. Bottle and seal.

Mulberry Jelly

500 g mulberries
500 g tart apples or crab apples
sugar

Cover the fruit with water and simmer until soft. Strain through a jelly bag. Add 1 cup of sugar for every cup of extract. Stir until the sugar is dissolved then boil briskly until setting test is reached. Bottle, label and seal.

Redcurrant jelly

500 g washed redcurrants
500 g sugar
1 cup water

Place all ingredients in a pan and bring to the boil, stirring until sugar dissolves. Boil briskly for 10 minutes. Pass jelly through a sieve, or blend. Let the mixture stand a few minutes, if blended, to allow the froth to settle. Remove froth with slotted spoon. Reheat to just boiling point. Bottle and seal. This jelly is a useful glaze for flans and fruit tarts. Just heat it gently until it is runny, and spread with a pastry brush.

Rose-hip Jelly

Rose-hips need to be gathered when they are bright red and fat, usually after the first frost. Rose-hip jelly is good with poultry and game. Brushed over the breast and back of game birds it gives a delicious tang to the meat.

1 kg rose-hips

sugar

pectin

Roughly chop the rose-hips. Put in a pan and cover with water. Bring to the boil and simmer until hips are pulpy. Strain through a jelly bag. Allow 1 cup of sugar to 1 cup of syrup. Stir the sugar into the juice and bring to the boil, stirring until sugar is dissolved. I find I need to add commercial pectin at this stage to get a nice firm jelly. I use citrus pectin (available from health food shops). Use 1 teaspoon for each kilogram of fruit. Make it into a paste with some of the hot mixture and pour into the pan stirring to make sure pectin mix is completely dissolved. If you are using liquid pectin follow the directions on bottle. Boil until setting test is reached. Bottle and seal.

Blackberry Jelly

500 g blackberries (2 punnets)

juice of 2 lemons

sugar

Wash and hull the blackberries. Put the berries, lemon juice and 1 cup of water in a pan and simmer until the fruit is pulpy. Strain through a jelly bag. Measure the juice and add 1 cup of sugar to each cup of juice. Heat gently, stirring until the sugar is dissolved. Boil until setting point is reached. Bottle and seal.

Elderberry Jelly

900 g elderberries
900 g cooking apples
sugar

Chop the apples roughly. Place them in a pan and cover with water. Simmer until the fruit is pulpy. Do the same with the elderberries in another pan. Strain the fruits together through the one jelly bag. Add 1 cup of sugar to each cup of syrup and return to the pan. Bring rapidly to the boil stirring until the sugar is dissolved. Boil until setting point is reached. Bottle and seal.

Lilly Pilly Jelly

quantity lilly pilly fruit
sugar
1 lemon
tartaric acid
water

Wash the fruit after removing the stalks and place in a pan with barely enough water to cover. Add the whole lemon and bring to the boil, boiling gently until the fruit is tender. The fruit will lose some colour. Strain through a jelly bag, muslin or fine milk-strainer. Do not squeeze fruit. Leave to strain overnight. The next day add 1 cup of sugar to each cup of liquid and 1 teaspoon of tartaric acid to each 6 cups of liquid. Boil till the jelly reaches setting point. Skim off the surface scum, pour the jelly into small jars and seal when cool.

HERB JELLIES

To make a batch of herb jellies make a quantity of this basic piquant jelly, adding various herbs at the bottling stage.

Basic jelly

This is a good way of using up windfall apples or crab apples.
2 kg apples or crab apples, with bruised parts removed
water to cover

Simmer the apples and water until the fruit is tender. Add 1 cup of white vinegar 5 minutes before the end of cooking. Drain. Strain through a jelly bag. Add only three-quarters of a cup of sugar for each cup of extract. Stir over a gentle heat until the sugar is dissolved, then boil briskly until setting test is reached.

Mint Jelly

Wash and chop finely 2 cups of mint leaves and add 5 minutes before bottling while the jelly is still very hot. Stir the mint into the jelly so it is evenly distributed. Mint jelly is wonderful with roast lamb or any lamb dish.

Rosemary Jelly

Wash and dry the rosemary. You can either strip the leaves from the stalks and add them to the jelly mixture 5 minutes before bottling as in mint jelly, or you can wash the sprigs of rosemary, cutting them long enough to stand up in the jars, then pour the jelly in around the sprigs. Seal and label.

Sage Jelly

Wash and dry the sage leaves and proceed as for rosemary jelly. This is lovely jelly with roast duck or turkey.

Thyme or Marjoram Jelly

Wash and dry thyme, marjoram, or a mixture of both, and proceed as for mint jelly. This is especially nice with roast chicken, and it makes a tasty glaze spread over the chicken in the oven minutes before cooking is completed.

The basic piquant jelly mixture, if divided into four portions, will give you several jars of each kind of herb jelly. Use small jars, so that, if you decide you like only one kind, you can make up the entire batch next time with only one herb. I like them all, and four little baby food jars of herb jelly tied up in cellophane with a ribbon and some sprigs of dried or fresh herbs makes a great gift of love from the garden.

*M*armalades

Richness, colour and form,
Ripe flowers and juices rare.
(Frank Wilmot)

Although there are recipes for marmalades made with quinces and exotic things like ginger, when most people think of marmalade they think of citrus: orange, grapefruit, lime, lemon, mandarin, cumquat, and combinations thereof. Marmalades mostly belong to the breakfast table but I can still remember from my childhood steamed puddings topped with marmalade which were tummy-warming and filling. Does anyone eat steamed puddings these days?

Marmalades have more water and sugar than fruit and so have a longer cooking time to get to the setting test. The best and easiest marmalades are slightly bitter. The added pectin in sour fruits like grapefruit, pomelos, lemons and cumquats helps them set well. It is possible to make a very good sweet orange marmalade but the fruit must be fresh and all the pips and white pith should be added in a muslin bag while cooking for extra pectin.

I once asked a group of about twenty older women for a good marmalade recipe. Almost all had one, they were all very similar, and each woman was prepared to swear that hers was not only unique but the best marmalade I would ever eat. Marmalade makers are not to be trifled with so I went home and sifted through all the recipes, compared them with my own and some in books. The similarities were there, yet the marmalades were all slightly different to taste.

Some marmalade recipes say to mince the fruit. Although this makes perfectly edible marmalade, it doesn't have the translucent effect that makes marmalade look and taste so special. Some people shred the skin, some slice it in with the pulp, some peel the fruit finely with a potato peeler and cut it up into slivers with scissors. It's all a matter of individual preference. There's a marmalade recipe here for every different way.

Some General Hints for Good Marmalade

Wash the fruit carefully, scrubbing gently with a brush to remove dust and grit from indentations on the skin. Cut skins as finely as possible whether shredding or slicing. Cut out as much of the white pith as possible. It makes the marmalade bitter and spoils the look of the finished product. Soak the skins and pulp overnight. Tie the pips and white pith into a muslin bag and soak with the skin and pulp. Pips are rich in pectin and will help the marmalade to set. Before adding the sugar, simmer the skin and pulp in the muslin bag with the lid on the pan, until skins are tender.

I have sometimes used cup measurements with these marmalade recipes. If you follow these recipes it is important that you use a cup of the same size for both fruit and sugar.

My Favourite Grapefruit Marmalade

2 grapefruit
2 lemons
water (about 1.2 L, enough to cover fruit)
sugar

Peel the grapefruit finely with a sharp knife so that no pith is taken. Slice the peel very finely and put in a basin. If you have a marmalade shredder, shred the peel straight into a plastic or ceramic bowl.

Peel the lemon and cut up the peel in the same way. Peel off all the white pith from both the lemons and the grapefruit. The more you take off the better your marmalade will look. Cut up the fruit as finely as possible and add to the peel in the bowl. Measure the pulp in a cup and for every cup of pulp add 3 scant cups of water. Put the pips and pith in a piece of muslin with a cotton tie long enough to dangle over the side of the pan. Leave to soak overnight.

The next day place the simmered fruit and water with the muslin bag in a pan and simmer until the skin is soft and the pith is transparent. Allow to cool long enough to handle and for every cup of mixture add 1 cup of sugar. Discard the bag of seeds and pith. Simmer and stir the marmalade until the sugar is dissolved, then boil rapidly until setting test is reached. Allow to cool slightly before bottling to prevent the fruit from rising. Bottle and seal.

My Mother's Sweet Orange Marmalade
My mother always used cup measures and valencia oranges. These are the summer oranges with pips, available in the shops from September.

4 oranges
2 lemons
9 $\frac{1}{2}$ cups of water
2 $\frac{1}{4}$ kg sugar

Cut up the oranges and lemons, cover with the water and leave to stand overnight. In the morning boil the fruit hard for half an hour then add the sugar and boil very hard for another hour (or until setting test is reached).

My mother's marmalade would set in an hour but mine isn't as well brought up and sometimes takes longer.

Pressure Cooker Marmalade
It is possible to reduce the cooking time of marmalade by doing the first process in the pressure cooker before the sugar is added. Put the rind, juice, water and the bag of pips and pith in a pressure cooker and cook for 20 minutes from when you switch on the heat. Allow to cool until the lid can be removed then add the sugar, remove bag of pips and pith, and stir until the sugar is dissolved with the lid off. Boil until setting point is reached. Bottle and seal.

Ginger Marmalade
500 g grapefruit
150 g lemons
100 g crystallised ginger

water

sugar

Squeeze the grapefruit and lemons, then put the ginger and citrus skins through the blender or cut up into small chunks. Put the pips in a piece of muslin and tie up tight. Put the juice, blended fruit and ginger in a pan. Add the same amount of water ,about 6 cups. Simmer slowly until the fruit is translucent and the skins are soft. Allow the mixture to cool a little and add 1 cup of sugar for each cup of pulp. Boil rapidly until setting test is reached. Stir in 1 teaspoon of ground ginger just before bottling. Bottle and seal.

Lime Marmalade

4 limes, ripe and juicy but not yellow

1 lemon

water

sugar

Peel the limes and lemon thinly with a potato peeler. Cut peel into fine slivers with scissors. Remove all white membrane and slice fruit thinly. Remove pips and place pips and membrane in muslin bag and tie up. Cover fruit with 2 cups of water for every cup of fruit and peel. Put bag of pips in and soak overnight. Next morning simmer gently until skins are soft and fruit is transparent. Remove bag of pips. Add sugar and boil rapidly until setting test is reached. Bottle and seal.

Cumquat Marmalade

Cumquat marmalade is different in flavour and texture from other marmalades. It is a gourmet experience. My cumquat tree is not yet in full bearing so my cousin Wendy steals them (with permission) from a tree in her street. We spend a friendly afternoon every winter making enough cumquat marmalade for us both.

1 kg cumquats

1 $^1/_2$ kg sugar

400 mL water

Wash and slice the cumquats and cover with water (approx. 400 mL). Remove the pips and place them in another bowl. Just cover with water (approx. 100 mL). Leave both bowls to soak overnight. The next day strain the pips from the water and add the water to the cumquats. Put all in a pan and simmer for about 20 minutes. Add the sugar, stirring until dissolved. Boil rapidly until setting test is reached. Bottle and seal.

Chunky Marmalade

3 oranges(choose thin-skinned oranges and lemons)
1 lemon or 2 limes
sugar

Slice the fruit up by cutting right across it, then cutting each slice in half or quarters if the fruit is large. Remove the pips and place them in a muslin bag. For every cup of pulp add 3 scant cups of water. Soak overnight then boil until fruit is tender and liquid is reduced by half. Put the muslin bag of pips in with the fruit while boiling. Remove the bag of pips and measure the pulp. For every cup of pulp add 1 cup of sugar. Boil rapidly until setting test is reached. Bottle and seal.

Three-fruit Marmalade

1 orange
1 lemon
1 grapefruit
water
sugar

Peel the fruit with a potato peeler and slice finely. Use a shredder if you prefer. Remove as much white membrane as possible from the fruit and cut up small, retaining all the juice. Put the pips and membrane in a muslin bag and tie up tight. For every cup of fruit, peel and pulp add 3 scant cups of water. Leave to soak overnight with the bag of pips and membrane. The next day put all in a pan and boil slowly until the skins are soft and the liquid in the pan is reduced by half. Remove the bag and discard. Add sugar to the pan, stirring until it is dissolved. Boil rapidly until setting point is reached. Bottle and seal.

Whisky Marmalade

Use the chunky marmalade or three-fruit marmalade recipe. When setting point is reached remove any scum from top and stir in 100 mL whisky. Stir the whisky into the marmalade and let it stand for a few minutes before bottling. Stir with a wooden spoon to distribute peel evenly. Bottle and seal.

Mandarin Shred Marmalade

1 kg loose-skinned mandarins
1 grapefruit
2 lemons
water
sugar

Peel the mandarins and slice the peel finely with scissors. Tie the finely shredded peel in a muslin bag. Wash and roughly chop the lemons and grapefruit. Put the mandarin segments and chopped fruit into a bowl. Cover with water, place the bag of peel in with the fruit and leave to soak overnight. The next day boil all until the fruit is soft and the liquid is reduced by half. Remove the bag of peel after 20 minutes. Pour all the fruit through a jelly bag, leaving it to drip awhile, then squeeze it to get all the juice. Discard the pulp. Add the sugar to the juice, stirring the sugar until it is dissolved, then add the peel from the muslin bag. Boil all together until setting test is reached. Allow to stand, then stir the peel evenly through the mixture. Bottle and seal.

Aunt Hilda's Prize-winning Marmalade

1 kg fruit (grapefruit or oranges)
2 $^{1}/_{4}$ L water
sugar

Shred or cut up the skin finely and place it in a bowl with enough of the water to cover it. Leave to stand overnight. Cut up the rest of the fruit, pips and membrane and soak these in the rest of the water overnight. The next morning, in two separate pans, cook both mixes until the fruit is soft. Cook the fruit longer than the peel. Strain the fruit portion through a jelly bag. Squeeze it as much as you like to get all the juice and pectin. Combine the juice and rind with one cup of sugar to every cup of juice and rind, and boil rapidly until setting point is reached. Bottle and seal.

Marmalade in the Microwave

It is really easier and less messy to make the marmalade the usual way but if you prefer cooking in a microwave here is a recipe for you.

2 oranges, or an orange and a lemon, or 10 cumquats

sugar to equal weight of fruit
juice of 2 lemons

Using a vegetable peeler or shredder cut the rind from the fruit. For the cumquats simply cut up the fruit finely leaving in the pips. Cut the rind into shreds and leave aside. Remove all the white pith from oranges or lemons and discard. Cut up the fruit or chop in the blender. Leave the pips in and place all in a large microwave-safe bowl. Cover with boiling water and microwave on high for 15 minutes. The fruit should be well blended. Put this through a sieve or Mouli-mill, leaving only the juice. Stir the shredded rind and sugar into the hot juice and microwave for 15 minutes, stirring every 2 minutes until the sugar is dissolved. Once the sugar is completely dissolved microwave again on high for another 10 minutes or until setting point is reached. You will need to check for the setting point as microwaves vary in voltage. You may need to cook the marmalade a little longer or cook it more quickly. Times vary with the amount of pectin in the fruit. Bottle and seal when cooked. For cumquats simply cut up the fruit finely, add sugar and lemon juice and microwave until cooked, stirring every minute until the sugar is dissolved. Remove the pips when cooked. They will float to the top. Bottle and seal.

Lemon Marmalade
1 kg ripe juice lemons
150 g sugar
2 L water

Wash the lemons well. Take off the peel very finely with a vegetable peeler. Cut into thin strips. (It is quicker if you use the kitchen scissors.) Remove as much of the white membrane as possible and put the lemons through a blender. Allow the mixture to settle and remove the pips. They will float to the top. Put the pips in a muslin bag with the membrane from the lemons. Put the bag, lemon pulp and peel in a pan and cover with water. Leave to stand overnight. Next morning simmer all together until peel is soft. Remove bag of pips. Add the sugar and stir until it dissolves, then boil rapidly until setting test is reached. Allow to cool slightly. Bottle and seal.

LEMON

Bitter breast
of the earth
I've picked this one
from a dark green laden tree

this is a cold hard
obdurate fruit
yet one swift act
releases the juice
enhancing oysters
fish and almost everything else.

the acerbic aunt
of the orchard
beautiful in youth
yet growing thorny
in old age
irritating
irritable

when I move house
the first tree I plant
is a lemon

biblical
dour and versatile
I much prefer it
to those cloying salesgirls
the soft stone fruits.

Kate Llewellyn

LEMONS

I must say something here about the versatile lemon. Like Kate Llewellyn the first tree I plant when I move house is a lemon. I have some friends who were country school teachers moving from school residence to school residence every few years. In the backyard of each house they occupied they planted a lemon tree. They knew they would be there only for a short time, probably not long enough to harvest their lemons, but they considered the trees a gift for others who would occupy the houses after them and hoped some day to get a house with a mature lemon tree. I don't know that they ever did, but I do know that when they eventually built their own house in Melbourne there was a lemon tree planted on their block of land even before the house was built.

It is a fruit that is useful in so many ways, and it is absolutely essential for adding acid to bring out pectins in fruits with low pectin content like strawberries, figs, apricots, peaches, pears and melons. I use lemon juice in almost all my jam recipes and frequently in pickles and relishes to bring out the flavour.

- Lemon juice is used to prevent discolouration of fruit when it is standing. Squeeze a lemon over peaches, nectarines, feijoas, kiwi fruit and bananas to stop them going brown.
- Lemons make good marmalades, and combine well with other citrus for mixed citrus marmalades.
- Lemons can be substituted for limes or lime juice in any recipe.
- Lemon juice can be used for deglazing a pan to provide the base for a sauce for meat and chicken.
- Lemons can be placed in the microwave and softened to make squeezing easier and extract more juice.
- Lemons can be pierced with a fork and squeezed gently if only a few drops or a teaspoon of juice is needed. The lemon will keep and can be used again.
- Lemon slices added to the pan when poaching fish improve the flavour.

- Lemons cut in halves or quarters and added to rice while it is steaming or boiling will enhance the flavour.
- Lemon rind, grated, gives a kick to cooked carrots or cauliflower or to batter for frying fish.
- Lemons are full of vitamin C and are great thirst quenchers.
- Lemon cordial can be made and stored. Home-made lemonade with just lemon juice, sugar and water is one of the simplest and best-loved summer drinks.
- Lemon slices in gin and tonic or a twist in a dry martini or other cocktails is one of the best ways to use them.
- Lemon juice can be frozen and used for drinks or cooking. Freeze the juice in ice-cube trays and, when frozen, tip them into plastic bags for storage.

CHAPTER FIVE

Butters, Cheeses and Curds

Let us get up early to the vineyards
Let us see if the vines flourish,
Whether the tender grapes appear,
And the pomegranates bud forth.
(Song of Solomon)

Fruit butters and cheeses are two parts of the one process. Fruit must be washed well, cut up and simmered until it is soft and mushy. It is then sieved or blended until it is a fruit purée. Sugar is added and the mixture is simmered until the required consistency is reached.

Cheeses, butters and pastes are made exactly the same way but the cheeses are cooked longer. It is a matter of reducing the fruit pulp to the required consistency. Butters are soft and spreadable. Cheeses set much firmer and can almost be sliced.

Fruit pastes, which should really be called fruit pastilles as they are nothing like a paste, take the process even further, being cooked until the mixture leaves the side of the pan. These are quite solid and can be cut into squares and stored in wax paper. They can be sliced and they look and taste tremendous on a cheese platter. They are also very good served with poultry or game. Damson or plum cheese is particularly good with duck.

FRUIT BUTTERS

Apple Butter
1 kg apples
200 mL water
200 g sugar
juice and rind of 1 lemon

Chop the apples roughly. Cover with water and simmer until tender and mushy. Stir through sieve or Mouli-mill. Return the purée to the pan. Add the sugar and the juice and rind of one lemon. Simmer, stirring frequently until the butter is the right consistency. Children love this simple apple butter.

Crunchy Apple Butter
Make apple butter as above. Just before removing the pan from the stove stir in 25 g finely chopped walnuts or 25 g slivered or chopped almonds. Remove from the stove and bottle immediately. Seal while hot. This is wonderful on dry biscuits with cheese.

Spicy Crab Apple Butter
This is a good breakfast spread for those who prefer something tangy and not so sweet.
3 kg crab apples
1.2 L water
1.2 L dry cider
1 teaspoon ground cloves
1 teaspoon ground cinnamon
1 teaspoon ground nutmeg
soft brown sugar

Cut the crab apples in half. Simmer in the water and cider until the fruit is pulpy. Stir through a sieve or Mouli-mill. Simmer the pulp until it is thick. Weigh the pulp and add 350 g sugar for each 450 g pulp. Stir in the spices and cook slowly, stirring frequently until the mixture is reduced and thick and there is no surplus liquid. Bottle and seal.

Grape Butter

500 g grapes
500 g sugar
2 tablespoons water

Combine all ingredients in a thick-bottomed pan (or use a mat underneath). Bring to the boil, stirring until the sugar is dissolved, then boil rapidly for 15–20 minutes. Sieve or blend the mixture. Return to the pan and bring to just boiling point. Remove from the heat. Bottle and seal.

Medlar Butter

Medlars will not ripen on the tree so pick them as soon as they are a good golden brown colour (if you don't the possums will) and bring them inside to ripen. I put them in a shallow wooden dish on the kitchen bench. I like to look at them; they are such a quaint little fruit. They must be soft and brown inside. Use only fully ripe fruit.

1 kg medlars
juice and rind of 1 lemon
300 mL water
sugar

Cut the medlars in half and simmer with the water until they are soft and mushy. Stir through a sieve or Mouli-mill till a purée is obtained. Add three-quarter cup of sugar for every cup of pulp. Simmer, stirring frequently, until the mixture is the consistency of cream. Bottle and seal.

Medlars were traditionally eaten by the gentlemen of Oxford with their port so you can eat yours at the kitchen table and consider what good company you keep.

Plum or Damson Butter

1 kg plums
150 mL water
sugar

Wash the plums and cut them in half or slice them from the stone. Add water and simmer gently until they are soft and pulpy. Put through sieve or Mouli-mill. Add 1 cup of sugar for each cup of purée. Simmer slowly, stirring constantly, until the mixture is the consistency of cream. Bottle and seal.

This butter will keep better than some others because more sugar is used. I use it to make plum muffins. Use any muffin recipe and just add a spoonful of plum butter when putting the muffin mixture in pans.

Pineapple Butter
450 g pineapple (1 large pineapple), diced
225 g green apple, diced
2 tablespoons lemon juice
150 mL water
sugar

Put the pineapple, apple, lemon juice and water in a pan and simmer until the fruit is soft and pulpy. Put the mixture through a sieve or Mouli-mill to get a purée. Return to the pan with three-quarter cup of sugar to every cup of purée. Simmer, stirring constantly until the mixture is thick and creamy. Bottle and seal.

This makes a good cake or pie filling as well as being delicious on scones or toast.

Apricot and Orange Butter
1 kg apricots
grated rind and juice of 1 large orange
sugar
100 mL water

Wash and halve the apricots. Add water, orange juice and orange rind. Simmer gently until the peel is soft and mushy. Stir through a sieve or Mouli-mill. Add three-quarter cup of sugar to each cup of fruit purée and simmer, stirring constantly, until the mixture is the consistency of thick cream. Bottle and seal.

Banana Butter
10 bananas peeled and sliced
juice of 2 lemons
150 mL water
450 g sugar
1/2 teaspoon mixed spice

Put bananas, lemon juice and water in a pan. Simmer gently until the fruit is soft and mushy. This can be put through a blender as there are no seeds or skins to eliminate. Add sugar and simmer gently until thick. Bottle and seal.

FRUIT CHEESES

Making fruit cheese is simply a matter of taking the butter-making process a step further and reducing the purée until it is so thick it will set firm when cooled. This stage is reached when you can scrape a spoon through the centre of the purée in the pan and leave a clean line through it.

I usually pot the cheese into small straight-sided soufflé pots. If you spray these thoroughly with cooking spray, or lightly oil them, the cheese will turn out and you can wrap it in muslin or vine leaves if you are making it for a gift. You can use the same recipe as you used for butter only with more cooking, or you can try other fruits. Here are some cheese recipes.

Damson Cheese
Damsons are small tart blue plums which in some parts of Australia grow wild along creeks. They are grown in home orchards too but the ones gathered from wild, self-sown trees have a much better flavour. They all make great jams, butters and cheeses.

1 kg damsons
200 mL water
sugar

Use the damsons whole. The stones can be lifted out as they rise to the surface during cooking or when sieving the fruit. Place the damsons and water in a pan and simmer until soft and mushy. Put the mixture through a sieve or Mouli-mill to make a purée. Reduce the purée for another 10 minutes before adding the sugar. Add three-quarters of a cup of sugar for every cup of fruit mixture and simmer, stirring frequently, until a spoon leaves a clean line through the mixture. Turn into lightly greased pots or straight-sided jars and seal. Cover the soufflé pots with cellophane jam covers. Cheeses actually taste better after a couple of months' storage. They look great turned out on a cheese platter.

Quince Cheese

1 kg quinces
water to just cover
sugar

Chop up whole quinces including the skin and core. Cover with water. Simmer until very soft and pink. Put through a sieve or Mouli-mill to make a purée. Reduce for another 10 minutes then add three-quarters of a cup of sugar to each cup of purée. Simmer until thick and creamy, stirring constantly. Bottle and seal as for damson cheese.

Blackberry Cheese

1 kg blackberries
450 g cooking apples
600 mL water
sugar

Cut up the apples roughly, including skin and cores. Wash the blackberries and simmer with the apples and water. Simmer until soft and mushy, then put through a sieve or Mouli-mill. Stir the purée for another 10 minutes to reduce it. Add three-quarters of a cup of sugar to each cup of purée. Simmer until cooked, stirring constantly. Bottle and seal when the mixture reaches the consistency of thick cream.

Plums, preferably damsons, can also be used in this cheese recipe in place of the apples to make a plum and blackberry cheese. If you have plenty of blackberries they can be used on their own.

Fruit Pastes or Pastilles

If you are prepared to watch the pot all the time you can take the cheese process a step further and make a paste or pastille by cooking the mixture till it is really thick and leaves the side of the pan. Turn it out into a shallow, greased cake pan. When it sets firm, cut it into squares. Dip the squares into icing sugar and serve as sweets. They can be wrapped individually in cellophane and stored.

Confession: Once, when my concentration lapsed, my quince cheese turned into paste. If this happens to you and your cheese sets too firmly, simply turn it out, slice it into squares and serve with a flourish.

FRUIT CURDS

The lemon butter and passionfruit butter our mothers made were really curds as they contain eggs and butter and are not a true fruit preserve. I guess curd didn't sound as good. I know it was always referred to as lemon butter.

Here are a few curd recipes. Once again this process is the same for all fruits and fruit combinations. It's much quicker than making fruit butters and cheeses but still must be stirred constantly. If yours does curdle, give it a burst in the blender and return it to the pan. It will be fine. Curds do not keep as well as butters and cheeses and must be kept in the refrigerator after opening. Small quantities made often are best if you have curd lovers in your family. Curds can also be made quickly and easily in the microwave.

Lemon curd
grated rind and juice of 2 lemons
2 eggs
220 g sugar
120 g butter
Cream the butter and sugar. Add well-beaten eggs, lemon rind and juice. Cook all in a double boiler or in a bowl on top of a saucepan of water until the mixture thickens, stirring frequently. The mixture should not be allowed to boil or it will curdle. Bottle and seal.

Lime curd can also be made with this recipe, using the rind and juice of 4 or 5 limes.

Grapefruit and Lime Curd
grated rind of 1 grapefruit
8 tablespoons grapefruit juice
grated rind of 1 lime
4 tablespoons lime juice

350 g sugar

4 well-beaten eggs

Put all the ingredients together in a double saucepan or bowl over hot water and cook gently until thick. Do not allow to boil. Stir frequently. Bottle and seal. Keep in the refrigerator after opening. This is a nice tangy one.

Mandarin Curd

4 large or 6 small mandarins

150 g sugar

100 g butter

3 well-beaten eggs

Remove the skins from the mandarins. Cut into fine slivers with scissors, making about 2 teaspoons. Squeeze the mandarins with your hands to extract the juice. Stir the pulp through a strainer to remove the seeds and pith. Put the juice, sugar, butter, eggs and the small amount of peel into a double saucepan or bowl over hot water and stir frequently until thick. Bottle and seal. Keep in the refrigerator after opening.

Orange Curd

grated rind and juice of 2 oranges

juice of 1 lemon

225 g sugar

100 g butter

2 well-beaten eggs

Combine all the ingredients in a double saucepan or bowl over hot water and cook gently until thick. Do not allow it to boil. Bottle and seal. Keep in the refrigerator after opening.

Passionfruit Curd

8 passionfruit

50 g butter

250 g sugar

3 well-beaten eggs

juice of 2 lemons

1 tablespoon of water

Combine all the ingredients and cook gently in a double saucepan or bowl over hot water until thick. Do not allow it to boil. Bottle and seal. Keep in the refrigerator once opened.

Blueberry Curd

250 g blueberries (1 punnet)
50 g butter
250 g sugar
3 well-beaten eggs

Wash the blueberries and cook in 1 tablespoon of water until soft. This can be done in the microwave. Strain and stir through a sieve. Put the fruit pulp and all other ingredients in a double saucepan or bowl over hot water and cook gently until thick. Bottle and seal. Keep in the refrigerator once opened. You won't need to keep it for long as children love it and it is especially nice on pancakes or crepes. Blackberry, raspberry or loganberry curd can be made in exactly the same way. Strongly flavoured berries make the best curd.

Curds in the Microwave

Use the recipes above. Place all the ingredients *except* the eggs in a bowl and microwave on high for 3 minutes. Stir twice during cooking. Add well-beaten eggs and beat into the mixture. Cook on *high* for 5 minutes or until the mixture is thick. Check and stir every 30 seconds while cooking. Allow to cool a little. Bottle and seal.

If you can get enough baby food jars with re-sealable lids you can fill these with curd and reseal them by putting them in a large saucepan with a fold of newspaper in the water to stop the glass cracking. Cover the jars with water and bring to the boil, simmer for 30 minutes. They should be well-sealed and will keep indefinitely.

CHAPTER SIX

Sauces and Pickles

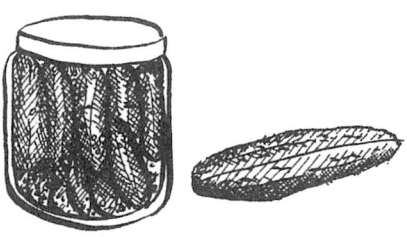

What is sauce for the goose may be sauce for the gander,
but it is not necessarily sauce for the chicken, the duck, the turkey or the guinea hen.
(Alice B. Toklas)

The most common time for pickling fruit and vegetables and making sauce is in the autumn, but it can be done in any season. Our forebears filled their foodstores with pickled fruits and vegetables when the raw ingredients were in abundance for eating in the seasons when there was nothing. In colder climates than ours, and before cold storage was understood, larders were filled in summer and autumn for the winter when snow lay thick and nothing grew. Every household put aside enough preserved food to see them through till spring.

In our bountiful country, with the best and cheapest fruits and vegetables in the overflowing supermarkets and markets, there is no real need to produce at home, but the joy of a full larder or cupboard of preserves made by one's own labour, with the flavour of the garden or orchards still about it, is something no supermarket product can match. So sterilise your bottles, lay in a supply of spices and sugar, collect your fresh ingredients and off we go . . .

SAUCES

Tomato Sauce

6 kg tomatoes
500 g onions
100 g salt
25 g ground cloves
25 g allspice
1 teaspoon ginger
1 teaspoon mustard
$1/4$ teaspoon cayenne pepper
1 kg sugar
50 g garlic
450 mL vinegar

Remove the skins from the tomatoes. (This is not strictly necessary, but so many tomatoes have tough skins that it makes the texture of the sauce better if you remove them.) Chop the tomatoes, skin and chop onions and garlic. Add all other ingredients and boil for one hour. Allow to cool a little, then process through a blender or Mouli-mill, or stir through a sieve. This will need to be done in batches. Return to the pan and boil again for 30 minutes or until the sauce is thick enough. Bottle and seal.

Green Tomato Sauce

3 kg green tomatoes
1 kg apples
500 g onions
225 g sugar
2 teaspoon ground pickling spice
$1/2$ teaspoon black pepper
1 teaspoon mustard powder
3 tablespoons salt
600 mL vinegar
2 teaspoons soy sauce

Peel and chop the tomatoes, apples and onions. Add all other ingredients to the pan and simmer gently for 2 hours. Sieve or blend the sauce, then return to the pan for a further half an hour, stirring frequently. Bottle and seal.

Easy Plum Sauce

$1\frac{1}{2}$ kg dark plums
750 g sugar
900 mL brown vinegar
3 teaspoons salt
25 g ground cloves
6 shakes cayenne pepper
30 g grated or chopped ginger

Wash and halve the plums. If the stones are very difficult to remove leave them in and as the mixture cooks the stones will rise to the surface and can be removed with a slotted spoon. Place all the ingredients in a pan and boil for 1 hour. Strain the sauce through a colander or Mouli-mill. Blend if you prefer a smoother sauce. Bottle and seal.

I always use small recycled soft drink bottles as the sauce is fairly thick and inclined to block up the bottle as it ages. This a good sauce to have on hand for pork, barbecues or Chinese dishes.

Mushroom Sauce

1.4 kg mushrooms
75 g salt
$\frac{1}{2}$ teaspoon black pepper
1 teaspoon allspice
$\frac{1}{2}$ teaspoon ground mace
$\frac{1}{2}$ teaspoon ground ginger
$\frac{1}{4}$ teaspoon ground cloves
600 mL vinegar

Cut up the mushrooms. Sprinkle them with salt and stand for several hours. Wash and drain the mushrooms well and combine with vinegar and spices. Simmer for about 30 minutes or until mushrooms are soft and mushy (sorry!). Put through a blender or sieve. Cool a little, then return to the heat and boil for 10 minutes, stirring frequently. Bottle and seal.

I am always a bit concerned about mushroom sauce keeping so I usually sterilise this sauce again. I put a wooden rack in the bottom of a deep pan and stand the bottles so they are not touching and are up to their necks in water. Simmer like this for half an hour with the lid on the pan. You can use thick newspaper to stand them on if you don't have a rack. I use recycled screw-top soft drink bottles. When the bottles are cold enough to touch screw the lids down tight again.

Blueberry Sauce

1 $^1/_2$ kg blueberries
2 large onions
2 large apples
350 g sugar
$^1/_2$ teaspoon ground cloves
$^1/_2$ teaspoon ground nutmeg
1 teaspoon ground ginger
1 teaspoon ground cinnamon
$^1/_2$ teaspoon salt
400 mL vinegar

Put the blueberries, the peeled and sliced onions and apples in a pan with half the vinegar. Bring to the boil and simmer until pulped. Pass through a sieve or blender. Return to the pan. Add spices, salt and the rest of the vinegar. Bring to the boil and simmer for 20 minutes or until thick. Bottle and seal.

Berry Sauce

This sauce can be made with loganberries, raspberries, blackberries or brambleberries. If you have a wonderful family day at a pick-your-own berry farm and don't want to make them all into jam, try this spicy sauce.

1 $^1/_2$ kg (6 punnets) berries
1 onion
1 apple
250 g sugar
1 teaspoon dry mustard
$^1/_2$ teaspoon ground cloves
1 teaspoon nutmeg

1 teaspoon cinnamon
1 teaspoon ground ginger
1 teaspoon salt
250 mL vinegar

Put the berries in a pan and mash with a potato masher. Add grated onion and apple, salt and spices. Boil all together until thick and blended, stirring frequently. Blend or sieve if a thicker sauce is required. If the berries are very seedy, sieve to remove the seeds. Bottle and seal.

Kiwi Fruit Sauce

2 kg kiwi fruit, peeled and chopped
6 cloves garlic
330 g sugar
300 mL white vinegar
2 teaspoons powdered ginger
1 heaped teaspoon freshly ground black pepper
2 teaspoons allspice
$1/2$ teaspoon cayenne pepper
2 teaspoons salt

Place all ingredients in a pan and boil for about half an hour or until the fruit is pulpy and well blended. Cool a little and blend or sieve the sauce. Return to the pan and boil again for 5 minutes, or more if the sauce is not thick enough. Bottle and seal.

Mango Sauce

8 ripe mangoes
600 mL white vinegar
440 g sugar
4 teaspoons salt
2 teaspoons curry powder
1 teaspoon ground ginger
1 teaspoon ground cloves
1 teaspoon pepper
1 teaspoon mixed spice
1 teaspoon nutmeg

1 teaspoon Worcestershire sauce
1 teaspoon chilli powder
10 cloves garlic
Peel and slice mangoes. Put all ingredients together in a large pan and simmer for 30 minutes or until mangoes are soft. Blend or sieve. Return to the pan and cook for another 10 minutes, stirring frequently. Bottle and seal.

Home-made Worcestershire Sauce

This is not strictly out of the garden except for the apple and lemon, but it is a good spicy sauce to use as a substitute for the bought variety.
$2 \frac{1}{4}$ L vinegar
125 g minced garlic
25 g cloves
1 kg treacle
10 g salt
25 g ground ginger
15 g cayenne pepper
6 whole pickling spice
1 sliced apple
1 sliced lemon
Place all ingredients in a pan. Bring to the boil and simmer for an hour, stirring occasionally. Let it stand for 24 hours and then strain, bottle and seal.

Mint Sauce

1 cup fresh mint, washed and chopped
400 mL vinegar
100 g sugar
Mix all the ingredients in a blender or chop the mint finely and mix with the vinegar and sugar. Boil hard for 10 minutes. Bottle and seal. This mint sauce will keep in a bottle.

The following sauces are not usually bottled. They are serving sauces that can be kept in jars in the refrigerator and are best used within a few days.

Horseradish Sauce

Mince 1 cup of grated horseradish with 1 cup of cream. Add half a teaspoon of salt and half a teaspoon of pepper. Mix well and serve with roast beef or with steak. It gives a brilliant kick to barbecued steak.

Sweet Mustard Sauce (for corned beef or pickled pork)

$^1/_2$ cup vinegar
$^1/_2$ cup corned beef water (the water in which the meat is cooking)
2 well-beaten eggs
1 tablespoon dry mustard
1 tablespoon sugar

Mix all ingredients together well and heat gently. Do not boil or the sauce will curdle.

Caper Sauce

1 cup of grated horseradish (or commercially prepared horseradish)
$^1/_2$ cup sour cream
2 tablespoons of drained capers, very finely chopped
1 clove crushed garlic
1 tablespoon gherkin, chopped

Combine all the ingredients and use with cold meats. Add a little mayonnaise and it makes a very nice sauce tartare for fish.

Curry Sauce

1 apple
1 onion
1 banana
1 dessertspoon of butter or margarine
1 dessertspoon of plain flour
1 tablespoon of curry powder
1 teaspoon of dessicated or grated coconut
1 cup of water, stock or milk
2 teaspoons lemon juice

2 teaspoons sugar
2 teaspoons chutney
salt to taste

Peel and chop the apple, onion and banana. Melt butter or margarine and gently fry the onion, fruit and curry powder for a few minutes. Stir in the flour and mix well, then add the milk or water or stock and stir until it boils and thickens. Add the salt, lemon juice, coconut, sugar and chutney. Simmer for 20 minutes, then strain. Store in the refrigerator. I use this easy curry sauce for curried pasta salad. It is equally good with prawns, crab or lobster but if you are using it for seafood use milk as the liquid.

MANGOES

mangoes are not cigarettes
mangoes are fleshy skinful passionate fruits
mangoes are hungry to be sucked
mangoes are glad to be stuck in the teeth
mangoes like slush and kissing

mangoes are not filter tips
mangoes are idiosyncratic seasonal seducers
mangoes are worse than adams apple
mangoes are what parents and parliaments warn against
mangoes like making rude noises

mangoes are not extra mild
mangoes are greedy delicious tongue teasers
mangoes are violently soft
mangoes are fibrous intestinal lovebites
mangoes like beginning once again

mangoes are not cigarettes
mangoes are tangible sensual intelligence
mangoes are debauched anti-socialites
mangoes are positive good in the world
mangoes like poetry.

Richard Tipping

Spicy Mango Sauce

2 mangoes, peeled and puréed
1 tablespoon Galliano or brandy
60 g butter
2 green chillies, finely chopped
1 teaspoon caraway seeds
salt and pepper to taste

Melt the butter in a pan and add all other ingredients. Whisk until smooth. Simmer gently until the mixture is smooth and cooked. If it is too thick add a little water.

This is not a sauce that will keep for a long period but it will keep for several days in the refrigerator and it freezes well. It is delicious served with chicken or pork or with a special curry.

A good way to use this sauce is to make mango chicken. Heat a portion of mango sauce, add an equal quantity of cream and pour this over sauteed chicken breasts. Garnish with fresh or canned mango slices.

To make mango chicken mayonnaise, combine mango sauce with the same amount of mayonnaise. Add an extra teaspoon of curry powder and stir in cold slices of chicken. This makes a good picnic dish or summer lunch.

Barbecue Marinade or Sauce

250 g butter or margarine
250 mL vinegar
250 mL water
125 mL tomato sauce
2 tablespoons Worcestershire sauce
juice of 1 lemon
1 tablespoon of dry mustard
1 tablespoons chilli powder
$^1/4$ teaspoon cayenne pepper
1 teaspoon freshly ground black pepper
1 teaspoon salt
50 g sugar
2 crushed bay leaves

2 minced garlic cloves
1 large grated onion
Melt butter or margarine. Add the vinegar, water, tomato sauce, Worcestershire sauce and lemon juice. Mix the mustard, chilli powder, cayenne, pepper, salt, sugar, bay leaves, garlic and onion together and add them to the mixture. Cook together, stirring gently for about 10 minutes. This sauce is excellent for marinating chicken or steak before barbecuing. You can also use it as a sauce over the cooked meat.

Freezer Tomato Sauce
This is a great way of using up tomatoes when they are plentiful and cheap. The sauce can be puréed when cooked or left chunky. I do some of each. I like the chunkier sauce on pasta. Combined with meat balls or grilled bacon pieces or with cooked sliced mushrooms it is a good basic sauce for any pasta dish. I sometimes use the puréed one for pasta but mostly I use it for spreading on a pizza base. I freeze some in family-size quantities and some in small quantities. I use these for tomato sauce or veal or chicken to make a parmigiana. It is one of my kitchen stand-bys. I have a tomato sauce day and get it all over in one go. Sometimes I buy a box of tomatoes from a stall or the market and I cook double this recipe; or you can make half if you want smaller amounts.
4 kg tomatoes
1 cup olive oil
8 onions chopped
2 carrots, grated or chopped small
half a stick of celery, de-stringed and chopped
12 cloves garlic or 1 heaped tablespoon garlic paste
4 bay leaves
salt and pepper
1 tablespoon sugar
1 teaspoon dried basil or 1 tablespoon fresh basil
1 teaspoon dried oregano or 1 tablespoon fresh oregano
1 small tub tomato paste (140 g)
small or large dash tabasco (or to taste)

Peel tomatoes by dropping them gently into boiling water for a few minutes. Remove from water and skins will come off easily. Heat the oil in a large pan and cook onions, celery and carrot till soft. Stir the oil through as they cook. Add the garlic just before removing from heat.

Mix all ingredients together and let simmer for 1 hour. Do not cook too quickly as you will lose the fresh tomato flavour. Cool slightly and blend to whatever texture you like or just put in containers and freeze. If you are only cooking half the mixture, halve the cooking time. If you are doubling the mixture, double the cooking time.

PICKLES

Vinegar is generally the preserving agent in pickles, chutneys and relishes. Some recipes call for slow cooking in brown or white vinegar with sugar and spices. Some call for blanching and draining of vegetables and fruit which is then cooked for a few minutes only, using a vinegar thickened with flour and flavoured with spices. Spiced vinegar is used in some recipes and while this can be bought already prepared it is a simple process and easy to make yourself.

A few important points
Vinegar is acidic and corrodes metal bowls, so use plastic or ceramic containers when soaking or blanching vegetables. Metal will also cause discolouring and change the taste of the product. For the same reason, pickles, chutneys and relishes should be packed into jars leaving at least 2 centimetres of space between pickle and lid. If metallic lids are used melted wax or a ring of waxed paper should be placed on top of the product between it and the lid. The flavour of pickles, chutneys and relishes develops better if the product is kept for two or three weeks before using.

Spiced Vinegar
It is easy to make spiced vinegar at home. Buy the type of vinegar you wish to use. There are many varieties although brown or malt vinegar is used in most sauces and chutneys. The vinegar is absorbed and blended with the other ingredients. White or red wine and cider vinegars offer a milder

flavour than the robust malt and are used with more delicate or specific fruit and vegetable pickles.

For spicing vinegar, spices can be tied in muslin bags and dangled into the pan while vinegar is heated. The vinegar is brought to the boil and simmered for 5 minutes, then cooled and the muslin bag withdrawn before bottling and sealing. If whole spices are used they can be boiled with the vinegar and removed by straining before bottling.

Spiced Vinegar 1
2 L vinegar
30 mL blades of mace
15 mL whole pickling spice
15 mL whole cloves
2 small cinnamon sticks
6 whole black peppercorns
2 dried red chillies (seeds removed)
1 bay leaf
Put the vinegar, spices and bay leaf in a pan. Bring to the boil and simmer for 5 minutes. Leave to cool, then strain through a fine sieve of muslin. Bottle and seal.

This is a fairly hot spicy vinegar suitable for pickled onions and chutneys.

Spiced Vinegar 2
1 L white vinegar
1 tablespoon whole cloves
1 tablespoon whole allspice
1 teaspoon nutmeg
1 small stick cinnamon
6 whole black peppercorns
Bring the vinegar and spices to the boil. Pour into a plastic or ceramic bowl and leave until cool enough to infuse. Bring back to boiling point. Strain out the spices. Bottle and seal.

Sweet Spiced Vinegar

1.7 L vinegar
250 g sugar
1 $^1/_2$ teaspoons salt
5 mL whole pickling spice
5 mL peppercorns
5 mL whole cloves
half a stick of cinnamon

Tie the spices in a square of muslin with light clean string or cotton. Bring the vinegar to the boil, stirring to dissolve the sugar. Add the muslin bag of spices and simmer for 5 minutes. Cover and leave to cool and absorb the spice flavours. Remove the muslin bag of spices and discard. Bottle and seal.

Any combinations of spices can be used, including chillies and garlic or herbs. Any method is suitable.

Curried Cabbage Pickle

1 large green cabbage
4 medium onions
50 g salt
1 L vinegar
$^1/_2$ cup flour
440 g sugar
1 tablespoon curry powder
1 tablespoon dry mustard
1 tablespoon turmeric
500 mL extra vinegar

Shred the cabbage and grate the onions. Place in a large plastic or ceramic bowl. Sprinkle with salt and leave overnight. Drain the cabbage and onions. Put them into a pan with 1 L of vinegar and boil gently until the cabbage and onions are soft (about 20 minutes). Mix the dry ingredients with the extra vinegar and stir into the pan. It should thicken quickly. Once it is thickened boil briskly for 5 minutes, stirring to prevent sticking. Bottle and seal.

Pickled Mangoes

500 g half-ripe mangoes
100 g salt
400 mL water
400 g raw sugar
250 mL white vinegar

Wash the mangoes and slice from the stone. Do not peel. Cut in lengthwise strips. Sprinkle with salt and let them stand for half an hour. Meanwhile boil the water, sugar and vinegar, stirring to dissolve the sugar. Put the mangoes into the vinegar mix and bring to just boiling point. Remove from heat and take the mangoes out with a slotted spoon and pack into sterilised jars. Pour the spiced vinegar over the mangoes in the jars. Seal and store in cool dark place for two weeks before using.

Pickled Grapes

1 kg grapes
1 litre spiced vinegar
200 g sugar
10 whole pickling spice

Wash the grapes and cut off the main stem leaving a small piece of stem attached. Make sure the skin of the grapes is unbroken and blemish free. Bring the vinegar, sugar and pickling spice to the boil and pour over the grapes in the ceramic or plastic bowl. Cover and leave them for two days, then pack grapes into sterilised jars. Bring the vinegar back to the boil again and boil for 5 minutes. Pour over the grapes. Cover and seal.

Tropical Pickle

1 pawpaw, peeled and finely chopped
1 cucumber chopped
1 kg peeled and chopped pineapple
1 kg ripe tomatoes, peeled and finely chopped
4 onions, peeled and finely chopped
250 g dates, stoned and chopped
250 g green beans finely chopped
vinegar to cover

220 g sugar

6 tablespoons flour

1 tablespoon turmeric

1 tablespoon curry powder

Place cut-up fruit in a pan. Barely cover with vinegar. Boil together for 20 minutes, stirring frequently to prevent sticking. Add the sugar. Make a paste of the flour and spices in a little extra vinegar. Stir into the boiling fruit and continue to simmer gently for 5 minutes stirring frequently until all the liquid is absorbed. Bottle and seal.

This was my standard pickle when I lived in the tropics. I sometimes used soursop or bananas instead of the pineapple. Mangoes can be used too or any combination of fruit as long as it makes up the same amount.

Pickled Blackberries

If you have lots of blackberries, and would like a change from sweet jams and jellies, pickled blackberries could be for you. They are delicious served with cold meats and poultry or added to a winter salad.

1 ^{1}/$_2$ kg blackberries

450 g castor sugar

275 mL brown malt vinegar

^{1}/$_2$ teaspoon ground cloves

^{1}/$_2$ teaspoon ground cinnamon

^{1}/$_2$ teaspoon ground nutmeg

Mix the vinegar, sugar and spices together and simmer for 5 minutes. Add the blackberries and simmer for another 15–20 minutes or until the fruit is just soft without losing its shape. Bottle and seal. Keep for two or three weeks before using.

Mustard Pickle

It took me years of practice to get this one right. The texture is important. The vegetables should not be overcooked. The time they spend in the hot vinegar mixture is the vital trick. Too long and they're soggy; not long enough and they don't keep well. Once you have the knack your pickles will be heaped with praise.

I use cup measurements for this one. If you have more onions than cucumber it doesn't matter, as long as the final amount is about the same.

2 cups cucumber, thickly sliced
2 cups chopped onions
2 cups cauliflower florets
2 cups sliced green beans
^{1}/$_2$ cup salt
5 cups water
^{1}/$_2$ cup flour
2 teaspoons dry mustard
1 teaspoon turmeric
^{1}/$_4$ teaspoon paprika
pinch cayenne pepper
^{1}/$_2$ teaspoon celery seed
1 cup water
^{1}/$_2$ cup sugar
2 ^{1}/$_2$ cups malt vinegar

Place the vegetables in a plastic or ceramic bowl. Sprinkle with the salt and add water to cover. Leave to stand for 24 hours. Pour off the brine and rinse the vegetables in cold water several times. Heat the vinegar and make a paste of the other ingredients with one cup of water. Add this paste to the pan when the vinegar boils, stirring until it thickens. Add the drained vegetables and just bring back to the boil. Remove from the stove immediately. Bottle and seal. Leave for 3 weeks before eating.

Mixed Mustard Pickles or Piccalilli

There are many recipes for piccalilli or mustard pickles, none of which vary greatly and all of which use the same process. Prepare your vegetables the same as for mixed pickles. Prepare the vegetables in brine and heat them in the brine to boiling point. Drain off the brine, return the vegetables to the pan (they should still be nice and crisp) and pour over them the mixture below. This is enough for about 3 medium-sized coffee or honey jars (350–500 g). If you need more, just double the recipe.

600 mL vinegar
1 teaspoon turmeric
$^1/_2$ teaspoon curry powder
2 teaspoon mustard
330 g sugar
$^1/_4$ teaspoon mixed spice
$^1/_4$ teaspoon cayenne pepper

Place all the ingredients in a basin and mix them together. Gradually add the vinegar, stirring until it is smooth. Pour this mixture over the drained vegetables and bring to the boil. Stir frequently to avoid sticking. Pour into sterilised jars and seal.

Pickled Plums

1 $^1/_2$ kg plums, not too ripe, but not green
vinegar to cover plums
same amount of sugar
1 cinnamon stick
6 cloves
$^1/_4$ teaspoon nutmeg
pinch of mace

Wash the plums and place in a basin. Pour over enough vinegar to cover. Pour the vinegar off into a saucepan, measuring as you go. For every cup of vinegar add a cup of sugar. Add spices, bring to the boil, and pour over the plums in a plastic or ceramic bowl. Let this stand for three days, then return to the pan, bring slowly to the boil and simmer for 10–12 minutes. Remove the plums from the pan and pack into jars. Cover with hot vinegar and seal. This is delicious in the winter with grilled sausages or any potato dish.

Pickled Onions

1 kg small round pickling onions
brine made of $^1/_2$ cup of salt for every 4 cups of water

Skin the onions and cover them with brine. Soak for 3 days, changing brine every day. Drain the onions and pack into hot sterilised jars. Put enough spiced vinegar to cover the onions in a saucepan and bring to the boil. Pour over the onions while hot. Bottle and seal.

Leave for at least 3 weeks before eating. Any spiced vinegar can be used for this recipe. More spices can be added straight into the jars if you want spicier onions.

Pickled cucumbers

330 g spiced vinegar
150 mL water
125 g sugar
25 g whole cloves
3 or 4 cucumbers, peeled, seeded and cut into 6–8 cm lengths.

Boil the vinegar, water, sugar and cloves. Add the cucumbers and boil for another 15 minutes or until the cucumbers are transparent. If you like the combination of dill and cucumber use a few sprigs of dill instead of the cloves.

Microwave Dill Pickled Cucumbers

small whole cucumbers (enough to fill a 1 L jar)
1 clove garlic, peeled
$1/2$ teaspoon dried dill or a head of fresh dill
$1/8$ teaspoon turmeric
1 small red chilli, seeded and finely chopped
300 mL water
100 mL cider vinegar
1 tablespoon salt

Place the washed and dried cucumbers in the jar with the garlic, dill, turmeric and chilli. In a microwave-safe jug or bowl combine the water, vinegar and salt. Microwave this on high for 4 minutes until boiling. Pour the liquid over the cucumbers until they are covered. Add additional water if needed. Cover the jar loosely with plastic wrap and microwave on high for 3 minutes. Leave plastic wrap on and seal with the lid. Store in the refrigerator after opening.

Note: You may need to cook the pickles a little longer, as some microwaves vary in temperature.

Pawpaw Pickles

1 small green pawpaw
500 g green tomatoes
3 cucumbers
2 onions
9 small chillies
5 teaspoons brown sugar
4 teaspoons curry powder
vinegar to cover all ingredients

Cut up the green tomatoes into small pieces. Sprinkle with salt and leave them overnight. The next day cut up the pawpaw and remove the seeds. Peel and seed the cucumber, cut it into small chunks. Cut up the onions, seed the chillies and slice finely. Leave the seeds in the chillies if you like a very hot pickle. Cover with vinegar, add curry powder and brown sugar. Boil until soft and all liquid has been absorbed. Bottle and seal.

Green Tomato Pickles

We live in a cold climate and our tomato plants are still left loaded with tomatoes by the time the first frost knocks them over. We pull up the whole plants and hang them in the shed. The tomatoes ripen slowly for a while but we always have a lot left green. This is a good way of using them up.

$2 \frac{1}{4}$ kg green tomatoes
1 kg onions
750 g sugar
$1 \frac{1}{2}$ L vinegar
1 tablespoon salt
1 teaspoon cayenne pepper
$\frac{1}{2}$ teaspoon ground cloves
$\frac{1}{2}$ teaspoon ground allspice
25 g turmeric
25 g mustard powder
100 g plain flour

Slice the tomatoes and onions. Sprinkle with salt and leave overnight. Strain. Combine the pepper, cloves and allspice with the vinegar (retain 1 cup of vinegar) and boil until nearly tender. Make a paste of the turmeric, mustard and flour with the extra vinegar and cook for a further 10 minutes or until the liquid is absorbed. Bottle and seal.

Watermelon Pickle

750 g white part of watermelon
800 mL water
150 g salt
300 mL cider vinegar
660 g sugar
1 tablespoon whole allspice
2 teaspoons whole cloves
2 small cinnamon sticks
1 small sliced lemon or lime

Cut the white watermelon rind into chunky pieces. Place it in a plastic or ceramic bowl. Mix the water and salt and pour it over the rinds. Leave to stand overnight. The next morning drain the rinds and rinse them several times. Cover with fresh water and bring to the boil. Simmer for 15 minutes or until becoming tender. Drain again and pat dry with a tea towel. Boil vinegar, sugar, spices and lemon or lime (tied in a muslin bag) together for 15 minutes, then pour over the rinds. Bring it all to the boil again and boil until the watermelon rind becomes transparent. Remove the rinds with a slotted spoon and pack into jars. Remove the bag of spices and lime or lemon. Cover the rinds completely with the syrup. Cover the pickle with wax or waxed paper if you are using metal lids. Seal and store in cool dark place for two weeks before using.

Pickled Crab Apples

500 g crab apples, washed, stems left on water to cover
110 g sugar
150 mL cider vinegar
1 teaspoon cinnamon
$^1/_2$ teaspoon ground cloves
1 teaspoon allspice
1 teaspoon ground ginger

Cover the crab apples with water and simmer until almost tender. Do not boil too fast or the skins will split. Add the vinegar, sugar and spices to the cooking water and simmer for 20 minutes or until the fruit is tender but still whole. Allow to cool slightly, then pour into hot, well-sterilised jars, trying not to break up the crab apples. Completely cover the crab apples with liquid. Seal and keep for two weeks before opening. Keep in the refrigerator after opening. These are delicious with cold meats.

Pickled Peaches

It always seems a shame to me to pickle peaches, but if you like spicy things and if you have lots of peaches here is a pickle recipe. Yellow peaches with firm flesh are best.

8 large yellow peaches, washed and sliced

400 mL white vinegar

500 g sugar

1 teaspoon cinnamon

2 teaspoons ground cloves

2 teaspoons whole cloves

Bring the vinegar, sugar and spices to the boil. Add the peaches and cook until they are soft but still firm. Lift the peaches from the syrup with a slotted spoon and pack into jars. Pour the liquid over the peaches, making sure all peaches are covered and there are a few of the whole cloves in each jar. Seal while hot.

Pickled Tamarillos

These are really scrumptious with meat (hot or cold) and make a beautiful sauce for roast beef or with beef Wellington instead of the usual mushrooms. They don't keep particularly well once the jar is opened. Use small jars with enough pickled tamarillos for one meal.

10 small tamarillos

150 mL white vinegar

220 g sugar

1 teaspoon ground cloves

$1/2$ teaspoon ground cinnamon

1 teaspoon grated lemon rind

Peel the tamarillos the same way as tomatoes. Drop them in boiling water for a second and skin will come off cleanly. The first time I made this pickle I left the skins on and it was bitter and horrible. Leave the tamarillos whole if your jars are suitable or halve or slice them. Put the vinegar, sugar, spices and lemon rind in a pan. Bring to the boil and add tamarillos. Simmer until the tamarillos are cooked but still firm. Lift the tamarillos out with a slotted spoon and pack into jars. Pour the hot liquid over and seal while still hot. Make sure all tamarillos are covered with vinegar.

Pickled Chokos

Chokos are so bland in flavour that they need a bit of hot stuff to give them a kick. Use chillies. Red if you like your pickles hot, green or yellow if you prefer a milder pickle.

4 chokos, peeled and cut into chunks
2 chillies, seeded and cut into strips
600 mL spiced vinegar
1 teaspoon salt
50 g sugar
2 whole pickling spice for each jar

Blanch chokos in boiling salted water and simmer for a few minutes until tender but still firm. Lift out with a slotted spoon. Bring the vinegar and chillies to the boil. Pack the chokos into jars and pour the spiced vinegar over them, making sure the choko is covered and putting 2 whole pickling spice in each jar. Seal while hot.

Pickled Bananas

12 under-ripe bananas
2 blades of mace or $^{1}/_{2}$ teaspoon powdered mace
6 whole cloves
300 mL spiced vinegar
350 g sugar

Heat the vinegar, sugar and spices in a pan, stirring until the sugar has dissolved, then boil briskly for 15 minutes. Peel the bananas and cut them into chunks or slice them lengthways if they fit your jar. Add them to the vinegar after it has boiled for 15 minutes and simmer until the bananas are just tender. Lift the bananas out with a slotted spoon and pack into well-sterilised hot jars. Strain the vinegar and pour over the bananas. Cover and seal.

Pickled Pears

1 ^{1}/2 kg firm pears (small ones are best)
1 cinnamon stick
25 g fresh green ginger
4 whole cloves
300 mL white vinegar
400 g sugar

Peel, core and quarter the pears and cook in water with a squeeze of lemon juice added until almost tender. Put the vinegar, sugar and spices in another pan, stirring until the sugar is dissolved. Simmer for 5 minutes. Lift the pears from the water with a slotted spoon and put them gently into the vinegar syrup. Simmer until the pears are translucent and very tender but not mushy. Lift pears out with a slotted spoon when they are fully cooked and pack them into warm well-sterilised jars. Turn up the heat under the syrup and boil hard for 5 minutes. Watch it carefully or it will boil over. If the phone rings turn it off. (I speak from experience here.) Pour the syrup over the pears and seal the jars. Keep them in a dark cupboard for 2 weeks before using. They are good with any cold meats and particularly good with a veal and ham pie or terrine.

Pickled Vegetable Sticks

These are very good to serve with dips or a cheese platter. If you cut the vegetables into sticks of uniform length you only have to open the jar to have a quick starter for unexpected callers.

3 cucumbers
1 large carrot, peeled
4 celery sticks, washed and trimmed
2 large red peppers, washed and seeded
100 g beans, trimmed and washed
450 mL vinegar
450 g sugar

1 tablespoon mustard seeds
1 teaspoon turmeric
This recipe takes 2 days to prepare. On the first day wash and cut the cucumbers into lengths to suit your jars. Leave them overnight in a brine made of 30 mL salt to 600 mL water. The next day drain and rinse the cucumber well and pat dry. Cut the celery, peppers and carrot into sticks the same length as the cucumber and cook in boiling salted water for 5 minutes for carrot, 2 minutes for other vegetables. Drain well. Place all the vegetables in a pan with the vinegar, sugar and spices. Bring to the boil. Boil for 1 minute, then pack the vegetables in jars and cover with the hot vinegar mixture. Seal.

Pickled Limes
18 limes scrubbed and dried and pricked with a sterilised darning needle
225 g salt
900 mL vinegar
600 g sugar
4 cinnamon sticks
30 mL whole allspice
15 mL cloves
Make a brine with the salt and 1 $^1/_2$ L of water. Pour over the limes and leave for 24 hours. Drain the limes and pat them dry. Place in a large pan. Add 2.8 L of water and simmer gently until the limes are tender. Put the vinegar, sugar and spices in a pan and bring to the boil. Boil for 5 minutes, then add the limes and simmer for 25 minutes. Lift the limes out with a slotted spoon and pack into jars. Strain the vinegar syrup and pour over the limes. Cover and seal.

Pickled Lemons
lemons
salt
spiced vinegar to cover
Peel the lemons and leave them whole. Small lemons are best. Dry-brine the lemons by putting them in a bowl or wide-necked jar, covering each layer with coarse cooking salt. Make sure they are well covered and leave for two

weeks until the lemons are soft. Shake and wipe off as much salt as you can and put the lemons into a clean glass jar. Heat the spiced vinegar to boiling point and pour over the lemons. Make sure they are completely covered. Cover and seal the lemons. Use the jars with plastic lids if possible or use a preserving jar with a glass lid and a rubber seal.

These whole spicy lemons give a piquant taste to braised or boiled meat or chicken. Squeeze them over rice dishes and curries or add them to the water when poaching fish.

Lemon Pickles

450 g ripe juicy lemons, washed and sliced and each slice quartered; save the juice, removing the pips
450 g salt
1 teaspoon chilli powder
2 teaspoons garam masala
75 g sugar

Pack the fruit with the mixture of spices and lemon juice into dry well-sterilised jars. This is a no-cook recipe so it is absolutely essential that the jars be clean and dry. Once they are full, leave the jars in the sun, turning frequently, for 2-3 days, giving them a good shake each day to distribute the sugar and spices. When the skins start to look translucent and tender the pickle is ready.

This pickle is very good with any dish cooked in coconut milk. Lime pickles can be made the same way and are just as good. I love the flavour and zing of limes and the Tahitian lime will grow and produce well in a sunny protected spot even in cold areas.

ACHARD

I first tasted these wonderful concoctions when we went to dinner with French friends in Vanuatu. Every French housewife in the tropics has her own special achard recipe. It is essentially a mixture of any fruit or vegetable pickled in oil instead of vinegar. It is always hot and spicy.

Lime Achard

36 limes
300 mL light oil (grapeseed, canola, light olive oil)
3 cloves garlic, sliced
1 teaspoon curry powder
3 small chillies
2 tablespoons salt

Cut the limes in half and remove the seeds. Cover them with hot water and boil for 2 hours until soft. Take them out of the water and allow to strain. Squeeze out the centre of the lime while it is hot. (You can squeeze this lime juice back into water and use it for blanching pawpaws for chutney.) Pack the limes into sterilised jars. Add curry powder, sliced garlic, chillies and salt to the oil and heat oil to the point where it just starts to smoke. Cover the limes in the jars completely with the oil. Seal while hot. The achard will be ready to eat in 24 hours.

Lemon Achard

lemons
salt
cooking oil
curry powder
garlic
whole pickling spice
chilli powder
saffron powder

Cut the lemons in half and place them in a bowl. Cover them with salt and leave for three weeks, stirring them every day. Wash the lemons thoroughly in fresh water and dry with a clean tea towel. Pour the boiling water over the lemons and soak for half an hour. Put them on a cloth to dry in the sun for a whole day, turning them from time to time. Take enough light vegetable oil to cover the lemons and add the spices. To every 500 mL oil add 1 teaspoon saffron powder, 1 heaped teaspoon curry powder, 3 crushed garlic cloves, 1 teaspoon pimento or pickling spice and $^{1}/_{2}$ teaspoon chilli powder. Heat the oil and spices for 10 minutes (but don't let it smoke), then stir the mixture through a sieve. Pour over the lemons, completely covering them. Cover and seal. Use plastic lids or glass with a rubber seal. If the achard is to be used quickly, and you have no glass or plastic lid, use a cellophane jam cover. Dip the cover in vinegar and place it tightly over the preserves. Seal with a rubber band. The cellophane will tighten as the vinegar dries. This pickle can be used in the same way as pickled lemons. It is a little hotter and spicier.

Green Pawpaw Achard
This is a recipe from my friend Gay in Vanuatu.

1 large green pawpaw
750 mL oil
6 seeded chillies
1 piece fresh root ginger
2 teaspoons curry powder
salt and pepper to taste

Peel and grate pawpaw and ginger. Chop the seeded chillies and combine them with the ginger and pawpaw. Heat the oil to just below smoking point and pour slowly over the pawpaw mixture. Allow the mixture to cool slightly, then add curry, salt and pepper. Spoon the mixture into the jars making sure all the mixture is covered. Use in two or three days. Keep in the refrigerator once opened, but it is best to allow it to reach room temperature before serving. It is very spicy and good with rice, meat, fish or vegetables.

*C*hutneys and Relishes

Chutney and relish – which is which? Some experts say ingredients for relishes are cut up small while chutneys are made of chunky-cut fruit and vegetables. Some say the opposite. In this book chutneys are made of cut-up fruit and vegetables, mostly without the use of flour for thickening, while relishes do have flour for thickening and are made of vegetables, mostly finely chopped.

CHUTNEYS

Apple Chutney
1 $\frac{1}{2}$ kg apples, peeled, cored and chopped
1 $\frac{1}{2}$ kg onions, skinned and chopped
450 g sultanas
grated rind and juice of 2 lemons
700 g sugar
600 mL white vinegar

Place all the ingredients in a pan. Stir until the sugar is dissolved. Simmer for 2–3 hours or until the mixture is pulpy. Bottle and seal.

This chutney can be put through a Mouli-mill or blender to get a finer consistency, then returned to the pan for 15 minutes and bottled while hot. It makes an excellent piquant apple sauce for serving with roast pork.

Crab Apple Chutney

1 kg crab apples
225 g onions
225 g light brown sugar
100 g sultanas
1 tablespoon salt
425 mL brown vinegar
1 tablespoon whole pickling spice
$1/2$ tablespoon dry mustard
1 teaspoon coriander seeds
2 pieces root ginger

Peel and core the crab apples. Mince or process the apples and peeled onions. Simmer in half the vinegar until tender. Add all other ingredients. Simmer until thick and all liquid is absorbed. Remove pickling spice and ginger. Bottle and seal.

Apricot Chutney

1 $1/2$ kg half-ripe apricots
450 g onions
1 teaspoon ground cloves
1 teaspoon ground allspice
$1/4$ teaspoon cayenne pepper
$1/2$ cup golden syrup or light corn syrup
600 mL vinegar
500 g sugar
1 dessertspoon turmeric
1 tablespoon plain flour

Remove the stones and cut up the apricots. Peel and dice the onions. Boil the vinegar, syrup, sugar, cloves, allspice and cayenne together. When boiling add the apricots and onions and cook until the fruit is soft. Blend the turmeric and flour with a little extra vinegar and add to the mixture. Stir carefully until the flour and turmeric is absorbed. Simmer for 10 more minutes. Bottle and seal.

Banana Chutney

900 g bananas, peeled and chopped finely
450 g seeded raisins
4 garlic cloves, skinned and finely chopped
2 red chillies, finely chopped
450 g brown sugar
2 tablespoons salt
4 tablespoons ground ginger
750 mL vinegar

Combine all the ingredients in pan and simmer until cooked and thick. Bottle and seal.

Choko Chutney

1 $\frac{1}{2}$ kg chokos, peeled and chopped
1 kg apples, peeled and chopped
450 g onions, peeled and chopped
450 g dark brown sugar
1 L wine vinegar
1 teaspoon ground ginger
1 teaspoon ground allspice

Place the choko pieces in a bowl, sprinkle with 2 tablespoons of salt and leave overnight. The next day rinse the choko pieces in clean water and drain. Place in the pan with all other ingredients. Heat gently, stirring until the sugar has dissolved. Boil gently for about 2 hours or until all the vinegar is absorbed and the chutney becomes thick. Bottle and seal.

Cucumber Chutney

1 $\frac{1}{4}$ kg cucumbers
750 g onions
2 cups sultanas

450 g sugar
3 teaspoons salt
1 teaspoon ground ginger
$^1/_2$ teaspoon ground allspice
$^1/_2$ teaspoon cayenne pepper
600 mL vinegar
Peel and slice cucumbers and onions. Add all other ingredients and simmer until thick and the liquid is absorbed, stirring frequently. Bottle and seal.

Feijoa Chutney
12 medium-sized feijoas
2 onions
2 green apples
250 mL vinegar
1 teaspoon mixed spice
1 teaspoon ground ginger
1 teaspoon ground cloves
1 teaspoon nutmeg
450 g sugar
$^1/_2$ teaspoon cayenne pepper
1 tablespoon salt
Wash and chop the feijoas. Peel and chop the onions and apples. Put all the ingredients in a pan. Bring to the boil and simmer, stirring frequently until the chutney is thick and all excess liquid is absorbed. Bottle and seal.

Fig and Tomato Chutney
1 $^1/_2$ kg tomatoes
1 $^3/_4$ kg figs
1 $^1/_2$ kg onions
1 $^1/_2$ kg brown sugar
500 g sultanas
6 cloves garlic
1 red chilli, finely chopped
2 tablespoons salt
1 tablespoon brown vinegar

Wash and slice the figs, tomatoes and onions. Crush the garlic. Add the sultanas and spices. Cover with vinegar and leave to stand overnight. The next day place all in a pan and cook steadily until the mixture is thick and all the liquid is absorbed. Bottle and seal.

Green Tomato Chutney

$1\ ^1/_2$ kg green tomatoes, thinly sliced
450 g apple, peeled and finely chopped or minced
225 g onion, peeled and minced
225 g sultanas
225 g brown sugar
2 teaspoons salt
450 mL malt vinegar
1 teaspoon chopped green ginger
$^1/_2$ teaspoon cayenne pepper
1 teaspoon mustard
Place all the ingredients in a large pan and simmer for about 2 hours or until the chutney is thick. Bottle and seal.

Kiwi Fruit Chutney

500 g kiwi fruit
2 large grated apples
1 clove garlic, skinned and chopped
175 g brown sugar
300 mL vinegar
$^3/_4$ teaspoon cinnamon
$^1/_2$ teaspoon ground cloves
$^1/_2$ teaspoon ground allspice
pinch chilli powder
100 g seedless raisins
2 onions, peeled and chopped
1 tablespoon crystallised ginger, finely chopped
Place all the ingredients except kiwi fruit in a pan and bring to the boil. Simmer for about half an hour or until the mixture thickens. Meanwhile,

skin and chop the kiwi fruit. Add to the mixture and simmer for another half an hour or until the chutney is thick. Bottle and seal.

Lemon Chutney

4 large lemons
2 large onions
250 g seeded raisins
450 g sugar
600 mL brown vinegar
2 teaspoons salt
2 teaspoons mustard seed
1 teaspoon cayenne pepper
1 teaspoon ground ginger

Wash and slice the lemons, removing all pips. Peel and chop the onions. Put into a bowl, sprinkle with salt and leave overnight. Place all the ingredients in a pan together, then simmer until tender and thick. Bottle and seal.

Mango Chutney

4 large ripe mangoes (do not peel)
1 teaspoon fresh root ginger, chopped
1 small green chilli, chopped
200 g brown sugar
300 mL brown vinegar
1 teaspoon ground ginger
1 teaspoon curry powder
2 garlic cloves, skinned and chopped
2 teaspoons salt

Place all the ingredients in a pan. Mix well and simmer for 1 hour or until all liquid is absorbed. Bottle and seal.

This is a mild chutney, excellent with curry.

Mango and Starfruit Chutney

3 large mangoes
3 large starfruit
45 g onions

2 garlic cloves
225 g sultanas or raisins
450 g sugar
500 mL vinegar
1 teaspoon curry powder
1 teaspoon ground ginger
1 teaspoon mixed spice

Peel and chop the mangoes, onions and garlic. Slice the starfruit. Add all other ingredients. Stir well and simmer for 1 hour or until all liquid is absorbed. Bottle and seal.

Pawpaw Chutney

Pawpaw trees bear fruit all year round. They are available in winter even in the southern markets.

2 kg pawpaw
250 g sugar
3 small chillies (less if you want a mild chutney)
1200 mL vinegar
2 teaspoons chopped fresh ginger
1 tablespoon cornflour
1 teaspoon mustard
1 dessertspoon mustard
1 dessertspoon turmeric
2 teaspoons salt
1 lemon or lime

Cut the pawpaw into chunks or strips and cover with water into which the juice of a lemon or lime has been squeezed. Leave to stand overnight, then drain well. Cover the pawpaw with water and cook gently for 10 minutes, then drain again. Leave the pawpaw to drain while all other ingredients are boiled together. Once the mixture is boiling stir in the drained pawpaw and cook for another 20 minutes or until the mixture is thick. Bottle and seal.

Peach Chutney

Peaches are my favourite summer fuit. I grew up in an orchard area and one of my sweetest childhood pleasures was to crawl under the hedge, away from my annoying brothers and a job-finding mother, with a good book and a lapful of peaches. Anzacs were my favourite variety; they still are. We have a tree in our garden.

2 kg peaches
500 g onions
250 g sultanas
700 g sugar
2 teaspoons salt
1 teaspoon white pepper
1 teaspoon ground cloves
900 mL white vinegar

Place all the ingredients in a pan and boil gently until the mixture is of a good consistency and all the liquid is absorbed. Bottle and seal.

Plum and Date Chutney

1.4 kg plums, halved, stoned and chopped
35 g dates, stoned and chopped
3 onions, skinned and finely chopped
600 mL malt vinegar
700 g sugar
1 tablespoon salt
1 teaspoon ground ginger
$^1/_2$ teaspoon black pepper
1 teaspoon nutmeg

Simmer the plums, onions and dates until soft. Stir in the sugar and spices and simmer until mixture thickens. Stir frequently while the mixture is cooking. Bottle and seal.

Quince Chutney

3–4 large quinces
2 large onions
250 g brown sugar
2 teaspoons salt
1 teaspoon ground ginger
1 teaspoon dry mustard

1 teaspoon curry powder
1 L malt vinegar
Cut the quinces and onions into chunks, cutting onions across the grain so that no rings are formed. Put all ingredients into a pan and simmer for 2 hours, stirring frequently, and mashing with potato masher as the quinces and onions soften. When the mixture is thick and all liquids have been absorbed bottle and seal.

Rhubarb Chutney
1 kg rhubarb, trimmed, washed and diced into small pieces
500 g apples, peeled and diced
500 g lemons, cut in half and sliced thinly
6 cloves garlic
2 tablespoons grated root ginger
2 tablespoons salt
800 g brown sugar
1 cup sultanas
1 cup seedless raisins
500 mL vinegar
Place the rhubarb and apples with sliced lemons and crushed garlic with the vinegar and spices in a pan and simmer gently until thick and all liquid is absorbed. Bottle and seal.

Tomato and Apple Chutney
1.4 kg tomatoes
1.4 kg apples
450 g onions
1 teaspoon powdered ginger
1 teaspoon pepper
1 rounded teaspoon salt
1 teaspoon ground cloves
1 teaspoon mixed spice
3 cloves chopped garlic or 2 teaspoons minced prepared garlic
900 g sugar
550 mL vinegar

Place all the ingredients in a large pan. Mix them together well and boil gently for an hour and a half or until the chutney is thick and all liquid is absorbed. Bottle and seal.

Tamarillo Chutney

30 tamarillos, blanched, skinned and chopped
4 large onions, skinned and chopped
4 large apples, peeled and chopped
1 cup dates, chopped finely
1 cup raisins, chopped
1 cup sultanas
1 teaspoon ground ginger
1 teaspoon cayenne pepper
2 teaspoons mixed spice
1 tablespoon salt
1.6 L vinegar
500 g sugar

Place all the ingredients in pan and bring to the boil, stirring until the sugar is dissolved. Simmer until the mixture is thick and all liquids absorbed. Bottle and seal.

Zucchini and Tomato Chutney

1.4 kg zucchini, peeled, seeded, cut into small chunks
450 g ripe tomatoes, skinned and chopped
225 g onions, skinned and chopped
2 teaspoons salt
2 teaspoons ground ginger
2 teaspoons freshly ground black pepper
1 teaspoon ground allspice
700 g sugar
750 mL vinegar

Place all the ingredients into a pan. Stir them together well. Bring to the boil and simmer for 1 hour or until the mixture is thick. Bottle and seal.

Hot Indian Chutney

700 g apples, peeled and chopped
450 g onions, skinned and chopped
700 g brown sugar
1.4 litres vinegar
450 g seedless raisins, chopped
4 large cloves garlic, skinned and chopped
4 teaspoons salt
2 tablespoons ground ginger
3 tablespoons mustard
2 tablespoons ground paprika
1 tablespoon ground coriander

Place all the ingredients in a pan and bring to the boil. Simmer gently until the mixture is thick and pulpy and all the liquid is absorbed. Bottle and seal.

Autumn Chutney

450 g plums
450 g apples
450 g tomatoes
450 g onions
2 large garlic cloves
450 g sultanas
600 mL vinegar
$^1/_4$ teaspoon mace
$^1/_2$ teaspoon mixed spice
$1\ ^1/_2$ teaspoons ground ginger
450 g sugar

Wash the fruit. Halve the plums. Peel and chop the apples and garlic. Skin and slice the tomatoes. Place all the ingredients except the sugar in a pan. Stir well and simmer for 30 minutes. Add the sugar, stir until it is dissolved, then simmer the chutney until it is thick and all the liquid is absorbed. Bottle and seal.

Mixed Fruit Chutney
This is a good winter chutney.
450 g dried apricots, washed, chopped and soaked in vinegar for 1 hour
450 g stoned chopped dates
700 g apples, peeled and chopped
450 g bananas, peeled and sliced
225 g onions, skinned and chopped finely
450 g sugar
grated rind and juice of 1 lemon and 1 orange
2 teaspoons mixed spice
2 teaspoons ground ginger
2 teaspoon curry powder
2 teaspoons salt
600 mL vinegar
Place all the ingredients in a pan and heat gently. Stir until the sugar is dissolved. Simmer until the mixture is thick and pulpy. Bottle and seal.

RELISHES

Corn Relish
For this recipe you will need enough ripe fat corn cobs to get four cups of kernels when scraped off with a sharp knife.
4 cups corn kernels
500 g onions, peeled and finely chopped
440 g sugar
220 g sultanas
1 red pepper, finely chopped
600 mL white vinegar
1 tablespoon salt
1 teaspoon turmeric
2 teaspoons dry mustard
3 tablespoons plain flour
Place the corn, onions and red pepper in pan with the vinegar, sugar and salt. Simmer until the corn is soft but not mushy. Add sultanas. Make a paste

with the flour, mustard, turmeric, and a little extra vinegar. Stir into the hot mixture. Cook gently for another half an hour. Bottle and seal.

Cucumber Relish

1 $^{1}/_{2}$ kg cucumbers
1 kg apples
1 kg onions
$^{1}/_{2}$ teaspoon cayenne pepper
1 dessertspoon turmeric
500 g sugar
1 tablespoon cornflour
750 mL vinegar
1 tablespoon salt

Cut up the apples, cucumbers and onions finely or put them through the food processor. Add vinegar, sugar, salt and cayenne pepper. Boil until tender. Make a paste with the cornflour and turmeric and a little extra vinegar. Add to the mixture and boil gently for a further 10–15 minutes. Bottle and seal.

Cucumber and Celery Relish

3 medium cucumbers, peeled, seeded and chopped
2 large onions, peeled and chopped
4 celery sticks, trimmed and sliced very finely
1 green pepper, seeded and finely diced
30 g salt
100 g sugar
2 tablespoons mustard powder
4 tablespoons plain flour
1 teaspoon turmeric
300 mL cider vinegar

Put all the vegetables in a pan with the vinegar and sugar and cook for 30 minutes, stirring frequently. Mix the turmeric, mustard and flour with a little extra vinegar and stir into the pan. Cook for a further 10 minutes. Bottle and seal.

Green Pawpaw Relish
1 green pawpaw, medium-sized, peeled and seeded
500 g green tomatoes
3 medium cucumbers, peeled, seeded and diced
2 medium onions, peeled and chopped
125 g brown sugar
1 tablespoon curry powder
$^1/_2$ teaspoon chilli powder
1 tablespoon flour
vinegar

Put all the ingredients, except the curry and chilli powder and the flour, in a pan. Just cover with vinegar and boil until soft. Put through a food processor on fine grater or blend lightly. Return to pan and stir in curry and chilli powder blended with the tablespoon of flour and a little extra vinegar. Cook for another 20 minutes or until the mixture is thick. Bottle and seal.

Lychee and Banana Relish
2 lemons, peeled and sliced
12 lychees, peeled, stoned and chopped
1 large banana, peeled and sliced
100 g preserved ginger, chopped
2 onions, skinned and chopped
225 g seeded raisins or sultanas
20 g salt
1 teaspoon ground ginger
$^1/_2$ teaspoon black pepper
300 mL vinegar

Boil all the ingredients together for an hour and a half or until the mixture is thick. Then mash roughly with a potato masher or put through the food processor. The mixture should not be too smooth. Bottle and seal.

Spicy beetroot relish
1 $^1/_2$ kg beetroot, lightly cooked
750 g onions
15 g brown mustard seeds

15 g horseradish, freshly grated, or the bottled commercial variety
700 g sugar
700 mL vinegar
4 tablespoons flour
Grate the cooked beetroot and onions. Add all other ingredients and boil for approximately half an hour. Mix the flour with a little extra vinegar and stir into the slightly cooled mixture. Stir thoroughly. Return to heat and cook for another 5 minutes, stirring all the time to prevent sticking. Bottle and seal.

Summer Relish
2 large carrots
1 green pepper
12 green beans
1 zucchini
12 cherry tomatoes
500 g cauliflower florets
300 mL wine vinegar
150 mL olive oil
12 green olives
30 g brown sugar
2 tablespoons chopped oregano
5 tablespoons watersalt and pepper to taste
Cut the carrots into julienne strips, pepper into small squares and beans into 1 cm lengths. Halve the tomatoes, stone and halve olives. Combine all ingredients and bring to the boil, stirring constantly for 5 minutes. Cool and bottle. Leave to marinate for a few days before opening.

Roadside Relish
Apple trees, elderberries and blackberries grow profusely on the sides of the roads where I live. That's why I call this one 'roadside relish'. I have to buy or grow the onions. Elderberries are not available all over Australia, but in Tasmania and some parts of Victoria, New South Wales and South Australia they are very common on roadsides and in gardens. This mixture of wild autumn fruits is put through the food processor so it has the texture

of relish without being thickened with flour. Strictly speaking it is probably a chutney. It goes well with roast chicken.

450 g cooking apples, peeled and chopped
350 g onions, peeled and chopped
700 g blackberries, washed and hulled
700 g elderberries, stripped off the stalks
600 mL white vinegar
1 teaspoon ground allspice
1 teaspoon ground cinnamon
2 tablespoons salt
$^1/_2$ teaspoon ground cloves
1 teaspoon black pepper
450 g sugar

Cook the apples, onions, blackberries, elderberries and spices in the vinegar, boiling for 20–30 minutes. Cool a little and put through the food processor, using the fine grater, or blend very lightly. Return pulp to the pan and add sugar. Stir over a gentle heat until the sugar is dissolved, then boil steadily for another 30 minutes or until mixture is thickened. Bottle and seal.

Tomato Relish

1 $^1/_2$ kg tomatoes, peeled
500 g onions
500 g sugar
1 tablespoon curry powder
1 $^1/_2$ tablespoons mustard
2 tablespoons flour
1 teaspoon salt
$^1/_2$ cayenne pepper
400 mL vinegar

Cut up the tomatoes and onions. Sprinkle with salt and let stand for several hours or overnight. Put in the pan, pour vinegar over the vegetables and add the sugar. Boil gently for one hour. Make a paste of flour, mustard and curry powder with a little extra vinegar. Add to the mixture and boil gently for another hour. Bottle and seal.

Fresh Rhubarb Relish

This is not a storing relish. It is made to be eaten straight away or will keep for two weeks in the refrigerator. It is great with a hot curry if you combine it with fresh plain yoghurt.

500 g rhubarb
3 thick slices of lemon
100 mL water
^{1}/4 teaspoon salt
110 g sugar
^{1}/4 teaspoon cinnamon
^{1}/4 teaspoon nutmeg
^{1}/4 teaspoon ground ginger
^{1}/4 teaspoon ground cloves
1 teaspoon grated lemon rind
^{1}/2 cup finely chopped mint

Cook the rhubarb and lemon slices in the water and salt until soft. Add the sugar and stir until dissolved. Strain off any excess liquid. The mixture should still be soft and mushy. Remove the lemon slices and stir in the spices, lemon rind and mint. Allow to cool and serve plain with curry of cold meats, or stir in with a little plain yoghurt.

Zucchini Relish

1 kg zucchini
4 large onions
1 red pepper
1 green pepper
125 g salt
500 mL white vinegar
200 mL water
2 teaspoons turmeric
2 teaspoons celery seed
1 teaspoon mustard seed

Chop the zucchini finely. Peel and chop the onions finely. Seed the peppers and chop finely. Put all vegetables in a plastic or ceramic bowl. Sprinkle with salt and cover with water and let them stand for two hours. Drain and rinse the vegetables several times. Put all the ingredients together in a pan and simmer until thick.

CHAPTER EIGHT

Drinks and Vinegars

Give me books, fruit, French wine
and fine weather, and a little music
out of doors, played by someone
I do not know.
(Keats)

CORDIALS, PUNCHES AND OTHER DRINKS

Rose Hip Syrup

Rose hips or heps are packed with vitamin C and many a baby of my generation was soothed with a bottle of diluted rose hip syrup. This recipe might be a bit sugary for modern babies, but the sugar is necessary as a preservative.

1 kg rose hips, topped and tailed

600 g sugar

1 $^1/_2$ L boiling water

Lightly blend the rose hips. Do not overblend or the syrup will be cloudy. Put the prepared rose hips into a plastic or ceramic bowl and pour over boiling water. Leave to stand for 20 minutes. Strain through a jelly bag. Add sugar to juice and bring to the boil stirring until sugar is dissolved. Boil gently for 5 minutes. Bottle and seal.

Note: The syrup will be a rather murky colour. If you add a few red rose petals to the mixture it will improve the colour.

Ginger Beer

When my children were small I always had a ginger beer plant muttering away on the kitchen window-sill, especially in summer, and it was a ritual as binding as the Sabbath that every seventh day we made ginger beer. Eventually we would get tired of making it and would have so many bottles stored we had to commit the unthinkable and throw out the ginger beer plant. My children now say to me: 'You can't write a book like this without including a recipe for ginger beer plant.' I had lost my old recipe but thanks to the patient research of my dear friend Toddy, here it is.

Ginger Beer Plant

Put in a screw-top jar:

8 sultanas

juice of two lemons

2 rounded teaspoons ground ginger

2 cups cold water

1 teaspoon lemon pulp

4 rounded teaspoons sugar

Put in a warm place for two or three days. When it starts to ferment (that is, starts to work) it will plop and gurgle a little. Quite exciting really. Once it looks as though it is starting to work, add every day for six days:

2 rounded teaspoons ground ginger

4 rounded teaspoons sugar

And on the seventh day . . . pour the plant into a bucket or large container and add:

4 cups sugar

4 cups boiling water

juice of 2 lemons

26 cups of cold water

Mix all ingredients together. Strain through a very fine sieve or through muslin or cheesecloth. Bottle and seal.

(*Important*: See the note about sealing bottles, below.)

Don't throw out the stuff left in the cheesecloth. Divide it in half and start another plant. Put it in a screw-top jar with 2 cups water, 2 teaspoons ground ginger and 4 teaspoons sugar. Feed daily with ginger and sugar as before for six days, then repeat the whole process until you and your family are tired of ginger beer, or summer has come to an end. The other half of the ginger beer plant can be thrown out or given to a friend who wants to go into ginger beer production.

Sealing the Ginger Beer Bottles

Every family who ever made ginger beer has a story about the bottles exploding. We used to store ours in the shearers' quarters and one very hot day a few bottles exploded, spraying ginger beer all over the beds. It was lucky it wasn't shearing time.

We used crown seals which you buy in a packet and hammer on with the hammer. Now there are quite a few screw-top bottles available. Bottles with metal screw-tops would be suitable but recycled plastic bottles have a strip seal which must be broken to open. These are not suitable.

The ginger beer becomes more volatile with high temperatures and with time, so stack your bottles in the sequence in which they were made, and first drink the longest-kept bottles.

Ginger Beer with Yeast

This recipe makes about a dozen full-size bottles.

12 L cold water
1 teaspoon tartaric acid
2 teaspoons cream of tartar
1 teaspoon lemon essence or juice of 2 lemons
1 teaspoon compressed yeast
1 tablespoon ground ginger
1 kg sugar

Dissolve sugar in some hot water. Dissolve yeast in half a cup of warm water. Put all ingredients in a large container, like a plastic bucket. Stir together thoroughly. Bottle and seal.

This will be ready in five days or longer, depending on how the yeast is working. Use crown seals or full screw-tops or bottles with wires holding the stoppers on, or you might have a minor explosion if you take a long time to drink all the ginger beer.

Citrus Cordial

rind and juice of 5 lemons
rind and juice of 2 oranges (or grapefruit if you like a tarter drink)
25 g tartaric acid
12 g citric acid
2 kg sugar
1 tablespoon Epsom salts

Put all ingredients except juice into a large bowl and stir till well combined. Pour over 1 $^1/_2$ L boiling water and stir till dissolved. Add juice. Strain and bottle. Use as cordial but keep in the refrigerator in a hot climate. There are any number of recipes for cordial but most require cooking and end up tasting like marmalade cordial. I prefer this one.

Pineapple Citrus Punch

This is a very good emergency drink for unexpected callers on a hot summer day, as everything except the lemon juice and mint leaves comes out of cans. It looks beautiful in a tall jug. Serve with lots of ice cubes. You can mix up the juices, lemon and tea and have them ready, adding the ginger ale and ice cubes when the thirsty horde is ready to drink.

juice of 4 lemons
1 cup of unsweetened pineapple pieces (with juice)
2 cups strong tea, chilled
500 mL orange juice
300 mL grapefruit juice
2 large bottles ginger ale

Mix together the tea, orange juice, lemon juice, grapefruit juice and pineapple. Chill in the refrigerator. Add ginger ale, ice and mint leaves before serving. Fresh fruit juice is even nicer of course. For a large bowl of punch I throw in the whole can of pineapple and juice, the whole bottle of orange and grapefruit juice, more lemon juice and tea. Mix it in a bucket or a big bowl. I use it like cordial and just add the ginger ale as needed to make up the quantity. Taste as you go to get it right.

For adult tastes, no sugar is needed. If you are making it for a children's party, use lemonade instead of dry ginger and add a few slices of banana.

Vegetable Cocktail

This is a good one for the morning after, and a good breakfast drink for dieters too. Substitute any vegetable to your taste. It sticks to your ribs all morning.

2 cups of tomato juice or 3 peeled tomatoes
pinch of salt
juice of 2 lemons
1 teaspoon Worcestershire sauce
1 small stalk celery, cut up and all strings removed
1 carrot, peeled and sliced
1 thin slice of onion

Blend all in blender till smooth. Dilute with a little water if too thick.

Apple Punch

3 large apples, peeled, cored and sliced
1 cup water
2 tablespoons brown sugar
1 teaspoon ground ginger
2 bottles sparkling cider (alcoholic or non-alcoholic)
1 bottle sparkling mineral water

Combine apples, water, ginger and sugar in pan and simmer till pulpy and cooked. Cool, purée in blender till very smooth. Chill. Place in a jug and add cider and mineral water or serve in glasses with apple mixture topped up with cider and mineral water. I use half-and-half.

Sparkling Champagne Punch

1 bottle sparkling white wine (need not be champagne)
2 bottles soda water or 1 bottle soda water and 1 bottle of lemonade
  according to taste
1 tablespoon castor sugar
1 jigger or small glass brandy
plenty of crushed ice

Simply combine all ingredients in a punch bowl or large jug and serve. Have all bottles very cold and punch can be made and served in a few minutes.

None of these punch recipes will be appreciated by wine buffs or serious drinkers. They are good, light alcoholic drinks for parties if people must drive home. You would need to drink half the bowl of punch to be over .05.

Sangria
This is a favourite summer drink, originally from Spain.

1 bottle of dry white wine
2 kiwi fruit, peeled and sliced
1 pear, sliced finely
1 cup fresh sultana grapes
2 tablespoons castor sugar
2 tablespoons brandy
3 tablespoons Cointreau
1 bottle plain mineral water

Pour wine into a large jug – it looks wonderful in a glass jug. Add fruit, brandy, Cointreau and sugar. Chill for 4–5 hours. Serve half-and-half with sparkling mineral water. If you don't have either Cointreau or brandy it is still a pleasant summer drink.

Black Sangria
This a dark-coloured drink and looks terrific in a white punch bowl. I use my large soup tureen.

1 bottle dry red wine
$^1/_2$ cup strong black tea
strip lemon peel
1 bottle sparkling mineral water
1 $^1/_2$ cups black or dark red fruit

Blackberries, loganberries or boysenberries, cherries or dark plums are good. Cut up plums but leave berries and cherries whole. Use a combination of fruit. Put fruit into jug and cover with tea and the red wine. Chill for several hours. Add mineral water and serve with ice and mint sprigs or pineapple sage flowers and leaves.

Both these drinks require only a very ordinary supermarket wine. Don't waste your vintage stuff.

Gluhwein

Not strictly fruity but a beautiful drink on a cold night. Serve with a ladle from a bowl which can be warmed or perhaps sat on a pot-belly stove or on the hob beside the fire.

1 bottle red wine
2 cinnamon sticks
4 whole cloves
large strips lemon and orange peel
sugar to taste

You can also add a slurp of brandy if you like, but the mulled wine is lovely without. Place all ingredients in a saucepan and bring to just below boiling pint. Remove from heat and cover it. Allow to stand for 10 minutes. Strain into a heat proof jug or bowl and serve hot.

Spiced Mulled Cider

2 bottles cider
1 tablespoon light brown sugar
pinch of salt
1/2 teaspoon whole allspice
large pinch of nutmeg
1 cinnamon stick
Large strip of orange peel

Mix all ingredients in a large pan and bring to just below boiling point. Strain and let stand for 5–10 minutes. Serve hot. This is equally good with alcoholic or non-alcoholic cider.

Spiced Perry

Spiced perry, or wine made from pears, can be made in exactly the same way as the mulled cider, but I use cinnamon instead of nutmeg and only a couple of allspice berries. The perry has a more delicate flavour than the cider.

Cumquat Liqueur

cumquats
brandy
sugar
pretty, sterilised jars or a wide-mouthed bottle
Scrub cumquats gently with a nail brush to remove any dirt particles in the skin. Prick all over with a sterilised darning needle. Cut off stems but leave a little green part on the skin. Pack cumquats into jars. For every 12 cumquats add 1 tablespoon of white sugar. Cover cumquats in jars with brandy. Screw lids on tight. Shake the jars every day until the sugar is dissolved. Hide in a dark cupboard for twelve months. Remove cumquats and rebottle liqueur. Use the cumquats for a special dessert with ice-cream and Savoiardi (sponge finger) biscuits.

Squeeze all the juice and brandy out of the rest of the cumquats to make a sauce. Add a little water to the brandy, heat and thicken with cornflour. Stir in 1 tablespoon of cream, and serve immediately.

Orange Liqueur

A liqueur similar to the cumquat liqueur can be made with oranges. I use it as a substitute for Cointreau and Grand Marnier in cooking. It is a bit messier than the cumquat recipe but very useful in the kitchen. You don't have to leave it as long as the cumquat liqueur before you can start using it, but it does improve with age even after the bottle is opened. I make it in a large jar with a rubber band and clip lid.
6–8 oranges, depending on size
brandy to cover
2 cups sugar (for a 1 L jar)
1 teaspoon cinnamon or 1 cinnamon stick broken into pieces
1 teaspoon ground coriander
Peel the oranges with a potato peeler, being very careful to avoid the white pith. Chop up the peel with scissors. Squeeze the oranges. Take orange juice, sugar and spices, stir well and place in jar with peel. Cover with brandy and leave in a dark place for 3 months. Strain, bottle and use with style.

Blackberry or Plum Vodka

This is a totally sinful and delicious way to preserve plums and blackberries.

Use elegant 1 L bottles and half-fill them with either blackberries or small plums (damsons or cherry plums). Pour half a cup of sugar into the bottle. You will need a funnel for this. Then fill the bottle with vodka. Seal the bottle and shake to dissolve the sugar. Shake every day for a week, turning the bottle upside-down each time. (Make sure it is sealed properly.) Hide at the back of the linen cupboard for three months, then strain off into a clean bottle. Leave for one year before drinking. And if you over-indulge because it is so delicious, please don't blame me.

Bellini

The best fruit/alcohol combination of all is a mixture of champagne and peach juice. It's an Italian invention called a *bellini*, presumably named after a Signor or Signora Bellini . . . blessings on her head.

To make it I open a bottle of champagne and pour a little in the blender. I peel a ripe white peach, remove the stone and blend champagne and peach flesh to get a liquid. Pour a little of this in a champagne flute. Using about the same amounts as you like for champagne and orange juice, top up the peach liquid with chilled champagne. *Magnifico!*

If you wish to prepare a large amount of peach juice and need to keep it for an hour or so, blend the peach juice with lemon juice and a little water and top up with champagne. This prevents discolouration.

VINEGARS

Raspberry Vinegar

Raspberry vinegar reminds me of Sunday school picnics when as children we sat around in a circle, each equipped with our own cup, and had it filled with raspberry vinegar poured from a large white enamel jug. We then had competitions, accompanied by much giggling, to see who could make the widest 'clown's mouth' with our raspberry-stained lips. Many a new dress, bought especially for the picnic, was daubed with raspberry stains from this messy exercise.

500 g raspberries (2 punnets)
600 mL white wine vinegar
250 g sugar

Make sure the raspberries are clean and contain no mildew or mould. Put into a plastic or ceramic bowl and cover with vinegar. Allow to steep for at least two days in a cool place. Stir now and then. Strain through a jelly bag and add the sugar. Heat to just below boiling point and simmer for 10–15 minutes. Allow to cool, then bottle and seal.

Herb Vinegars

Herb vinegars are easy to make and good to have in the pantry cupboard to add a bit of 'kick' to a recipe. There are hundreds of herbs and herb combinations you can use. I use two or three and find them sufficient for household needs. Herb vinegars have a marvellous flavour and improve salads and mayonnaise in the summer, and marinades all year round. It is most important that the bottles you save and use for herb vinegars are carefully sterilised and have non-metal lids. I save bottles with plastic or plastic-lined lids and refill them as I need them. I use only one bottle of each herb vinegar at one time and when it is finished I make another. The one I use the most is a mint vinegar with added spices. I use this in mayonnaise and salad dressings.

Spicy Mint Vinegar

^{1}/2 cup chopped and washed mint
^{1}/4 cup chopped chives
1 small red chilli with the seeds taken out
1 teaspoon peppercorns
1 L white vinegar

Put all herbs and spices in the bottle and fill with warmed vinegar. Seal and leave to marinate for two weeks before straining and returning to jar. Once you have made this vinegar in these proportions you can experiment with other flavours. I always take the seeds out of the chilli as they are so strong the chilli flavour drowns the other flavours, but you can add more or less herbs and spices to suit yourself.

Confession: Actually, I don't even measure the herbs and sometimes don't even cut up the chives and mint. Purists may shudder, but as long as the herbs, spices and vinegar marinate long enough, and the flavours blend, what does it matter?

If you are still using mother's old recipe for salad dressing made with condensed milk, vinegar, mustard and salt, try using this vinegar and beat in two eggs and you'll find the old favourite tasting more like a gourmet product.

Lavender Vinegar

Lavender vinegar is made by placing 2 teaspoons of lavender seeds in a bottle. Warm enough vinegar to fill the bottle. Cover and seal. Let the lavender steep in the vinegar for several days, then strain out the seeds and re-bottle the vinegar. This vinegar can be added to fruit salad to prevent browning of fruit and makes a nice vinaigrette.

I also make garlic vinegar which I use for marinades and for deglazing the pan when cooking chops or chicken breasts. I use red wine vinegar for garlic vinegar and leave the garlic in without bothering to strain it. We are garlic lovers in my house and the more garlic flavour it gets the better.

Garlic Vinegar

Put 5 or 6 garlic cloves (depends on the size of the bottle) in the bottom of a sterilised bottle. Fill it with warm to hot wine vinegar. Cork and leave for two weeks to marinate. Strain vinegar and remove garlic if you want a mild vinegar or leave the garlic cloves for as long as you like. You can strain and replace the garlic with fresh cloves when they start to look a bit soggy.

Note: In hot climates vinegar and herbs are more inclined to ferment if not properly sterilised or sealed. To prevent this you can simmer the vinegar and herbs for about half an hour. Strain the herbs from the vinegar. Bottle and seal. You can leave the herbs if you wish, or even add a sprig of fresh herbs.

Vinegars can be made with almost any herb and vinegar, or combination of each. Here are a few suggestions.

- Rosemary vinegar, made with white wine vinegar and rosemary sprigs or leaves.
- Thyme and cider vinegar
- Chive or shallot vinegar, made with chopped chives or shallots and wine vinegar. I combine a tablespoon of oil with a tablespoon of this, shake it together in a jar and pour over salad.
- Tarragon and white wine vinegar. Note that French tarragon has a milder flavour than Russian tarragon.
- Dill and white wine vinegar – mixed with a tablespoon of sour cream this makes a simple sauce for fish.
- Basil and white wine vinegar

HERB OILS

Herb oils are extremely simple to make, although you may need to experiment a bit to get the strength of the herb flavour you prefer in the oil. There is no need to use virgin olive oil; the cheaper, lighter oils are fine. The herb flavour overshadows the lovely olive oil taste. I like olive oil so I use light olive oil but canola oil, peanut oil or any good quality vegetable oil is suitable.

The simplest way is just to wash and dry the required herb and place it in a bottle. Either use a large sprig or, if you want a stronger oil, chop the herb finely and put plenty in the bottle. Warm the oil so that it will pour better and extract the herb flavour more quickly. Pour over herbs in bottles. Fill the bottles, put lids on, and leave in a warm place or on a sunny window-sill where the sun will help to extract the herbal essence. Leave for a few weeks, turning the bottles upside-down occasionally. Strain off the oil, pressing out any oil left in the herbs, and re-bottle. The longer you leave the herbs, the stronger the herb taste in the oil will be. If it is a bit wishy-washy after one process, don't despair, just repeat the process until you get the amount of flavour you want.

If you want to have a decorative row of herbal oils in your pantry or on a shelf, place a fresh sprig of whatever herb you used in the bottle, after straining the oil. If you use rosemary it is a good idea first to dry out a bit of the oil in the microwave. Rosemary is rich in oil and it can get a bit overpowering if left too long. It also makes the oil a bit cloudy. Garlic can be used in the same way as herbs and a combination of rosemary and garlic oil is wonderful to rub over a piece of lamb or beef before roasting.

Lavender Oil

Place 2 teaspoons of dried lavender in a bottle and fill it with warmed oil. Allow it to stand in a sunny place for two or three weeks, then strain and seal. Made with baby oil this is a good bath oil or massage oil, a gift greatly appreciated by elderly ladies.

CHAPTER NINE

Drying, Crystallizing and other Country Kitchen Secrets

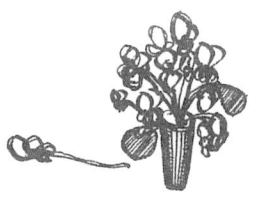

What is paradise? But a garden,
an orchard of trees and herbs
full of pleasure and nothing
there but delights.
(William Lawson)

DRYING FRUIT

Drying fruit at home the traditional way is not difficult. It takes a bit of time to prepare but warm air does the rest while you are getting on with other things. The trickiest part of drying things in my experience is keeping the dust off them. Apples dry beautifully in the kitchen on a piece of dowel or curtain rod. I once hung them in the kitchen on hooks but they accumulated dust and all the cooking flavours. It is essential to find a spot with good air circulation which is always warm and as free as possible of dust and odour. My best drying spot turned out to be the upstairs bedroom with the apple rings strung on sticks between the beds. It is best to remove them if you have visitors, especially if they are nearly dry, as the visitors eat them!

Apples are easy. They can be cored and strung on sticks. Pears, plums and apricots are not so obliging. I spread them on a special tray made of a wooden frame with fly-wire. My son-in-law made this for me when he saw me using an old window fly-screen. The screen allows the air to circulate well. You could stretch cheesecloth or muslin over an old picture frame if you are doing only a small quantity. This also makes them portable. I try to start the fruit in the sun. I put the trays outside on hot days and bring them in at night or if it rains. The moisture in the night air undoes all the drying of the day.

Drying Apples

Use unblemished fruit if possible. Peel and core apples and place in brine for 5 minutes to prevent discolouration. Make the brine from 50 g salt dissolved in 5 L of water. Drain well and dry on a cloth. Turn over and dry the other side. Thread apple slices on to dowel or curtain rod. Put outside for the first day but not in the sun. Under a veranda in a good breeze is ideal. Bring them inside at night and dry in an oven which is cooling down. If the oven is too hot the apples will shrivel and cook so watch them carefully. An airing cupboard or a warm room is a good place to dry apples. Continue in this way until the apples are leathery. When dry cool the fruit and pack into a box between layers of white paper. Use as dried fruit or reconstitute with water and use for cooking.

Drying Pears

Peel the pears. Cut in halves or quarters if very large. Place in brine made of 50 g salt dissolved in 5 litres water for 5 minutes to prevent dis-colouration. Drain well and spread on a cloth. Pat dry and spread on a frame made of fly screening or cheesecloth stretched over a frame. Place outside in the sun to dry. Bring in at night. Turn daily until the fruit is dry as for dried apples. The process can be hastened by putting pears on a rack in a cooling oven. When dry and leathery pack in boxes with white paper between layers or hang in paper bags in a cupboard.

Drying Plums or Apricots

Do not peel the fruit. Cut them in half and remove the stones. Place on racks, cut sides up and dry in the sun or a cooling oven as for apples and pears. When dry store in paper bags or boxes with paper between layers.

Dried Grapes

Sultanas, currants and raisins are simply three different varieties of grapes dried in the sun. Dry them on an airy rack in the same way as dried apricots or pears, remembering to bring them in at night.

Dried Figs

Figs can be dried by cutting them in half and proceeding as for dried apricots and plums. If the figs are left whole they take longer but are even more delicious. The small squat brown figs can be dried sitting on their bottoms with the stalk pointing up. When dry they can be strung on a cord and hung in the pantry.

Sun-dried Tomatoes

Tomatoes can be dried by the same method as fruit if the weather is hot enough. They lose flavour and colour if dried too slowly. I have a special method for sun-drying tomatoes in the colder areas. I take a white polystyrene fruit box and fill it to within about 10 cm of the top with scrunched-up newspapers. I cover this with a sheet of aluminium foil to make a heat reflector. I cut the tomatoes in half (use Roma or other small pear-shaped tomatoes) and lie them close together on the foil, cut-side up to start. Place in the sun, moving the box around to get maximum sunlight all day. Bring the tomatoes in at night or if it rains during the day. Keep in a warm dry place overnight and put out again the next day. Repeat this process until tomatoes are dried but not too shrivelled. Pack them into a jar with herbs of your choice. Basil or rosemary and garlic are a good combination. Cover with oil, making sure tomatoes are completely covered. Cover jars and store in cupboard or refrigerator.

One kg of Roma tomatoes will fill the foil surface on the box and make one small jar of sun-dried tomatoes. Don't throw the oil away when the tomatoes are used, use it for cooking or in salads. If the weather is not good and your tomatoes are not drying quickly, when you bring them in at night, place them in the oven at 100°C and leave them overnight. Put them in the sun during the day and the oven at night and they will be done in 2–3 days. You can of course do them completely in the oven but then they are not sun-dried tomatoes.

Kamaraden or Fruit Leather

This was a summer holiday task when my children were young. Armed with Grandma's old mincer and buckets of apricots and nectarines we would set up a trestle in the backyard and go into production. These days I would use a blender and do smaller quantities.

2 kg fruit (stone fruit and pears work best)

5 g potassium or sodium metabisulphite (available inexpensively at chemists)

Put fruit through a blender or food processor and stir in the metabisulphite. Spread fruit in a sheet on a clean plastic tray and dry in the sun. Bring in at night. Fruit should be $1^1/2$ - 2 cm thick; the thicker the better, though it does take longer to dry. After two or three days, when the fruit is beginning to solidify, turn the sheet over and continue to dry. When dry and leathery, cut into squares or strips and store in a jar or tin. A good healthy alternative to lollies and much appreciated for school lunches.

There are domestic food dehydrators on the market which are excellent for drying fruit, vegetables, herbs and seeds. They can also be used for making cottage cheese and yoghurt. They are reasonably priced if you are drying large quantities of produce, and they are powered by electricity. The dehydrator simply removes the moisture from the food by exposing it to warm dry air. It is the same process as drying in the sun or the oven. They do not take up a lot of room on the kitchen bench and can dry up to 11 kg of produce in a day. They come with comprehensive instruction books. Foods dried without preservatives or chemicals are useful for diabetics and those on special diets who have allergic reactions to preservatives and artificial food colourings. When you dry your own produce by whatever method, you know that no preservatives have been used.

DRYING HERBS AND FLOWERS

Plant material for drying should be picked in the middle of the day when the sun has extracted all the moisture formed overnight. Choose a warm dry day. Hang the herbs in bunches in a dry airy place out of the sun but where the air will circulate freely around them. A verandah is ideal. The herbs should be dry enough to harvest in two to three days depending on the weather. They should be paper dry and feel brittle. Run your fingers down the stems to harvest the leaves. Place a basin or tea towel underneath to catch the herbs. They should crumble in your fingers.

Place the herbs in warmed, completely dry jars and keep in a dark place. Dried herbs left out on a shelf will still be suitable to use but will lose some of their colour.

Drying Roses

Roses can be dried the same way as herbs. Pick the roses in bud. Remove all but a few leaves and hang them by their stems in a cool airy place to dry. When properly dried, rose stems will be brittle and can be arranged in a basket or base. The less time they take to dry the better the colour will be so choose your drying day carefully.

When drying rose petals and other herbs for pot pourri, detach the petals from the rose and spread them on clean paper (not newsprint as the print contains acids which destroy the perfume). Leave them in a warm room to dry. Drying frames used for drying fruit and vegetables can also be used.

Roses and herbs can also be dried in an electric dehydrator in the same way as fruit and vegetables.

Drying Herbs and Flowers in the Microwave

Herbs and flowers dry well in the microwave but because microwaves differ in voltage and every type of flower has a different moisture content the process is mainly a matter of trial and error. Place flowers or herbs on a paper towel and try one minute at a time on high. If they turn brown and start to cook try the next lot at a lower temperature and for a shorter time. You will soon work out the best way to proceed. Plants will vary in drying time on different days and at different stages of their development.

Lavender

I have a hedge of lavender around my herb garden and people who come to the garden often ask what I do with it all. I make lavender vinegar, lavender oil, lavender biscuits, pot pourri, sleep cushions, and moth preventers and then I use up the stems for firelighters. It is a very versatile plant.

I dry lavender by hanging it in long bunches upside down in a pillow-case. I used to hang it in bunches from a rafter but found I lost most of the flowers and seeds, so now I use old pillow-cases. The lavender flowers and seeds drop into the bottom of the pillow-case and are easily gathered.

I use most of the dried lavender for making lavender bags which I keep in wardrobes and linen presses. I have plenty of lavender, so I make quite large bags and they *do* keep moths out of clothes. The wretched little munchers chewed a hole in the skirt of my favourite black knitted dress a few years ago and I vowed I would not let that happen again. I hang bags of lavender from the rail in the wardrobe and lie flat bags of it between jumpers and woollies and in the linen cupboard. In summer I put precious woollies into pillow-cases with lavender bags and tie the tops with ribbon. The clothes-munching moths have admitted defeat and gone elsewhere.

I also use lavender seeds and flowers to make sleep pillows. A small pillow filled with lavender and tucked under the pillow on the bed helps even the most hardened insomniac to get some sleep.

I hang large bunches of lavender, still on the stem, in the loo and stand seeds around in small bowls. The rest of the seeds I use for pot pourri.

I use the stems from the lavender to make firelighters. I take the long dry stems and tie with wool up and down the whole length to make a wand of dry lavender that ignites easily and burns long enough to get the fire started. It also makes the room smell terrific.

I make my own pot pourri using lavender, dried rose petals and sweet-smelling leaves and flowers. I have tried lots of complicated recipes for pot pourri over the years and have now decided to stick with my own 'Tumbler's Green' recipe. Here it is.

'Tumbler's Green' Pot Pourri

First gather your rose petals, lavender, scented petals and leaves. Pick the roses and lavender when fully open and very dry. Remove rose petals from calyx and spread on dry paper, an old fly-screen, tightly stretched muslin or something similar.

Lavender, eau de cologne mint and any bunchy leaves or flowers can be tied and hung upside down over a wire or rail. Do not try to dry them wherever condensation may occur. Rosemary leaves take longer to dry than most others.

Everything used in pot pourri must be *very* dry. Your pot pourri may develop mould unless everything is paper dry. Dry in the shade to preserve colour and perfume. Check and turn the herbs every day. Some flowers and herbs will lose colour no matter what you do but try to keep them as bright as possible. Herbs and leaves should be rubbed through the hands into small pieces. Lavender can be pulled down the stem and into a paper bag or basket. Now you are ready to make your brew.

Use a glass, china or earthenware container with a lid. Never use plastic except in direst necessity. The hydrocarbons in the plastic will absorb all the essential oils. Spread a layer of dried petals and leaves mixed together in the bottom of the container. My rule of thumb is about 3 handfuls of dried material to 1 dessertspoon of orris root and 10 drops of rose geranium oil. Sprinkle 1 dessertspoon of orris root on each layer of dried leaves and flowers. Add the 10 drops of oil, and repeat until the container is full. Cover and leave for three weeks, stirring occasionally or giving it a shake. After three weeks you can place it in an open bowl or container and you will have the perfume of your garden for years.

If the perfume begins to fade place the whole bowl of pot pourri in a warm spot (on top of the television will do) or seal up for a few days, shaking often. A few more drops of oil added will renew the perfume of the pot pourri. If you like a spicy pot pourri you can add dried citrus peel, cloves, bay salt, cinnamon, allspice, rosemary or dried, crumbled bay leaves. The orris root and flower oils are usually available from gift shops, health food shops or chemists.

CRYSTALLISED OR CANDIED FRUIT

Crystallising and candying are similar processes. They are simply means of preserving fruit by impregnating it with sugar. You can take the process as far as you like depending on how much sugar you want and how long you can stand having bowls of sugar and fruit hanging around the kitchen. To get the full crystallised effect you may need to keep the process going for up to two weeks.

Preserved Orange Peel
This is a low-sugar recipe.
12 oranges
110 g sugar
75 mL water
Cut oranges into quarters. Remove peel in quarters. Eat the oranges! Don't cut peel into strips as large pieces retain their moisture better. Cover the quarters of peel with cold water and bring to the boil. Drain and shake off excess water. Do this 6 times (yes, 6 times!), then drain well and pat dry. Make a sugar syrup in a pan just large enough to take the peel. If it is too open the syrup will boil away too quickly. A saucepan with sloping sides is ideal. Put sugar and water in pan and bring to the boil. Boil very gently for 5 minutes, then add peel. Simmer the peel, turning pieces of skin gently to absorb the sugar. Skin can break easily. When all the liquid is absorbed remove from heat, lift peel gently out of the saucepan and leave to dry on a foil-covered tray that has been sprinkled with sugar. It will take several days to dry and should be put in a cupboard away from dust and flies. When dry enough to handle cut quarters into strips. Dip up to half-way in melted chocolate. Allow to dry for another day and store in a jar or container with an air-tight lid. These are great with coffee.

Crystallising Fruit – the Whole Process
This process is suitable for pears, peaches, pineapples, figs or quinces. The process of crystallising takes days of draining and adding sugar. Always do different types of fruit separately. Weigh the prepared fruit before starting.

For every 450 g fruit use 175 g of sugar and 1 L of water to make a syrup.

Stir the syrup until the sugar is completely dissolved. Bring to the boil and pour over the fruit in the bowl. Leave to soak for 24 hours. The next day pour off the syrup, return to the pan and add another 50 g of sugar for every 450 g of fruit. Dissolve the sugar by stirring gently. Bring to the boil and pour over fruit again. Repeat this for another 5 days, getting the syrup stronger every day. On the final day add 75 g of sugar instead of 50 g, and dissolve the sugar by stirring gently. Return fruit to the syrup on the stove and simmer for 5 minutes. Remove the pan with fruit and syrup from heat and stand for 4 days. Finally, drain off the syrup and spread the fruit to dry on an aluminium-foil-covered tray. Turn fruit often as it dries. This will take 4–5 days. When dry enough to handle, place between grease-proof paper in boxes or in jars.

For a crystallised finish, dip the fruit quickly into boiling water, using tongs. Drain, and roll in more sugar.

For a glacé finish, make another batch of syrup using 450 g sugar to 150 mL water and boil for 1 minute. Put a little at a time in a small bowl. Have a pan of boiling water beside it. Dip the fruit one piece at a time, first in the boiling water for 20 seconds then in the syrup for 1 minute. Use the syrup in small amounts as it becomes cloudy once the fruit has been dipped. Place on a foil covered tray to dry, turning often. Pack into containers between sheets of waxed or grease-proof paper or wrap individually.

Crystallised Flowers

Small flowers, like violets, primroses and the tiny pansies called 'Johnny jump-ups' are good for crystallising and can be used to decorate special desserts or *petit fours* and other small cakes.

Wash the flowers (heads only) and allow to dry completely. Beat an egg-white with 3–4 drops of rosewater. Paint the flowers with this mixture, using a tiny brush. Make sure you cover the entire surface of the flower, front and back. Then dip the flowers gently in castor sugar and shake off any surplus. (I use tweezers for this.) Leave overnight to dry. They will not keep long, so use them only for special occasions. Small, delicate leaves can be done in the same way.

COULIS

A coulis is a sauce made from fresh fruit or sometimes vegetables, usually containing a smidgin of liquor. It can be served hot or cold. A sweet coulis is wonderful with ice-cream and lady finger biscuits, with crepes and waffles and on puddings. It will last for several days in the refrigerator but will need to be frozen for preservation. No cooking is needed and a fresh raspberry or kiwi fruit coulis is a handy thing to have on standby in the freezer. I make them when I have perhaps only a handful of berries or one or two kiwi fruit or tamarillos going soft on the fruit bowl. They are simple if you have a blender.

Coulis takes the terror out of unexpected guests. You can always send the kids out for ice-cream and a packet of exotic biscuits. You will have your guests falling about with admiration when you serve ice-cream on a large flat plate with a berry or mango coulis, biscuits and some curled chocolate or other fruit. You can use any liqueur you have. I use Galliano for mango or peach coulis, Cointreau or Grand Marnier for berries and pears or citrus, but brandy is fine if you don't have these, and vodka will do at a pinch. Don't be too heavy-handed though, or you will spoil the fresh fruit flavour.

Berry Coulis
1 punnet berries (any type of berry is suitable)
1 cup sugar
1 tablespoon Cointreau
Blend all together and use in three days or freeze.

Mango Coulis
1 or 2 mangoes
sugar to taste
Galliano to taste
Blend all together and use in three days or freeze.

Vegetable Coulis
Vegetable coulis usually requires a little cooking to get the vegetables tender enough to blend. Any vegetables can be used. Steam or microwave them to get them just right. Soft juicy vegetables, like tomatoes and spinach,

require little added liquid. You can create your own coulis by adding a bayleaf or some garlic or onion for flavour plus a dash of vinegar or wine to get the flavour you want.

Parsnip Coulis

Once, when I had four or five people to feed and only enough parsnip for two, I made this parsnip coulis in a hurry and served it with roast beef and Yorkshire pudding.

1 parsnip, peeled and diced
half a potato, peeled and diced
1 clove garlic, peeled and finely chopped

Cook parsnip and potato till just tender in about half a cup of water. It can be done (covered) in the microwave. Blend with half a cup of white wine and the garlic. Add pepper and salt to taste. Stir in half a cup of cream or sour cream and reheat, but do not allow to boil or the cream will curdle. (The potato was really only to make the parsnip go further. It would be better with two parsnips and without potato.)

Green Vegetable Coulis

Use asparagus, spinach, peas, beans, broccoli, snow peas (or *mange tout*) or a combination. Broccoli and spinach are a bit strong to mix as their flavour overpowers the others, but used on their own or with a little onion or garlic they are splendid.

75 g green vegetables, lightly steamed
75 g butter for cooking vegetables

Sauté in butter till tender. Blend and add 300 mL cream, white wine or both, as needed to get the consistency right. Add salt and black pepper to taste.

Avocado Coulis

1–2 avocados
yoghurt
garlic
lemon juice

Blend together in quantities to get pouring consistency. This depends on the size of the avocados. This is a cold coulis to serve with a chicken salad.

AVOCADO
Slicing open green flesh
my fingers encounter a
smooth brown shiny egg
glistening in the sun
like old polished wood
seeming unbreakable

yet left on the windowsill
in bright sunlight its skin
becomes brittle, cracks open
revealing shrivelled insides

we too become old
our traitorous bodies
revealing hidden decay

Susan Perry

Tomato Coulis
6 ripe tomatoes, chopped
1 tablespoon tomato paste
1 carrot, chopped
1 bay leaf
Put tomatoes, carrot, bay leaf and herbs in a saucepan with just enough water to cover. Cook gently until water is reduced by half. Strain or blend, adding the tomato paste . . . and your coulis is ready. This one is nice hot or cold. I use it hot on veal schnitzel and chicken breast, and cold on terrines and vegetarian dishes.

OTHER COUNTRY KITCHEN SECRETS

Roasted Garlic Paste
If you have an abundance of garlic (it grows wild all over the place here), or it is on special at your local market or greengrocer's, try this garlic paste. It keeps indefinitely in, and for several days out of the refrigerator.

10 bulbs of garlic
one-third of a cup of water
2 tablespoons olive oil
This makes about one cup of garlic paste. Remove the outer skins of the garlic (the loose papery ones) and put the garlic cloves in a greased oven pan, pour over the oil and water. Cook garlic in a moderate oven until it is soft (about 1 hour). When garlic is in the oven, baste it occasionally with oil and water and add a bit more water if it dries up. When cooked allow to cool. Press the garlic out of the skins into the food processor and blend until smooth, or mash with a fork. Store in a jar in the fridge. For a few weeks you won't have to peel and crush garlic: just use a spoonful of this in pasta and rice dishes, with vegetables and bread. If you like your steak garlicky this is also a great way to use it.

Figs in Wine
1 kg fresh figs, firm and well-coloured but not squashy ripe
225 g sugar
300 mL water
grated rinds of 1 lemon and 1 orange
450 mL light red wine (Rosé or Beaujolais are perfect)
1 teaspoon ground cloves
You will need a large deep pan. Put the sugar, water, cloves and peel on to simmer, stirring till sugar is dissolved. Let simmer for a few minutes then add the wine. Poach the figs gently in the wine syrup for a few minutes. You may need to do this in batches depending on the size of your pan. Lift figs out gently with a slotted spoon and pack into well-sterilised jars. Pour the syrup from the pan over them, completely filling the jars. Seal tightly. We usually eat some of these as soon as they are made and bottle the rest. Once you open the jar keep in the refrigerator.

Brandied Plums, Cherries or Cumquats
All equally sinful and delicious, and very expensive to buy, these brandied fruits are cheaper and more fun to make. They are handy to have in the cupboard to make a quick dessert and are particularly nice with ice-cream and Savoiardi (sponge finger) biscuits and curled or grated chocolate.

Select firm, fresh fruit. Prick cumquats all over with a sterilised darning needle. Pack tightly into jars covering each layer of fruit with a layer of sugar – not smothered, just covered. Fill all jars this way, then cover all with brandy. Put lids on tightly and shake every day until sugar is dissolved, then put them away at the back of the cupboard and leave for at least three months. I save my prettiest jars for these. With handwritten labels, a ribbon and a sprig of dried lavender they make lovely gifts.

Fruit Candies

These are great for school lunch-boxes or nibbling in front of the TV. This recipe is based on sweetened fruit pulp. Use ripe fruit and chop roughly. Add enough water to prevent sticking and simmer till soft, mashing from time to time to extract the juice. Stir through a sieve or Mouli-mill. Here you can add sugar or not as you choose. A little artificial sweetener added at this stage makes the sweets suitable for low sugar diets. They seem, however, to need some sugar for the taste and as a preservative. Simmer the sweetened pulp, stirring frequently until very thick and reduced. Then spread out on muslin stretched over a wire rack and dry slowly. This may take several days depending on the weather. Don't put it in the sun, dry it slowly indoors. When firm enough to handle cut it into squares or strips and dip in coconut or castor sugar. Store in containers between layers of waxed or grease-proof paper.

Candied Angelica

If the angelica in your herb garden has invaded the rest of the bed, get your revenge by cutting it down before it flowers and seeds and use the young angelica stems to make this lovely candy. You can use it a as a sweet or add it to rhubarb dishes where it gives a very special flavour. Use it for decorating cakes too.

quantity of young angelica stems cut into 10 cm lengths
100 g salt
sugar
water

Place in a plastic or ceramic bowl in a shallow layer. Mix salt with enough boiling water to cover and blanch the angelica. Pour over and leave for 24 hours. Lift angelica pieces from brine and cover with cold water in a bowl to prevent drying out while you make a syrup of 600 mL water and 700 g sugar. Boil the mixture for 10 minutes, then add the drained angelica pieces and boil for another 20 minutes. Lift out angelica and dry on a rack for 2–4 days. Store syrup in refrigerator while angelica is drying. After 4 days boil angelica again in the syrup for 20 minutes and leave to cool in remains of syrup. Lift them out and drain for another 4 days. Toss them in castor sugar and store in air-tight container. They make lovely gifts in a pretty jar.

Peanut and Honey Candy
1 cup crunchy peanut butter
2 cups of full-cream powdered milk
$^1/_2$ cup coconut
1 cup honey
1 tablespoon chopped peanuts or chopped mixed nuts
Mix peanut butter and honey in a bowl. Stir in powdered milk, coconut and chopped nuts. Form into balls and roll in extra coconut or finely crushed peanuts. Refrigerate till set and firm. Store in screw-top jar. These fruit candies packed in plastic containers or pretty tins make good Christmas gifts.

A Spicy Sachet
A great gift for a friend who loves to cook, this is a sachet designed to cover up cooking odours. Although I rather like the house to smell of jams and preserves, I must admit the smell of lamb chops grilling is rather pervasive, and cabbage always reminds me of school food. To get rid of unwanted smells you boil one of these spicy sachets in a saucepan of water. Turn it off when it boils and let the smell permeate the kitchen. It will fill the room.
50 g whole cloves
25 g fresh bay leaves
15 g nutmeg
15 g chopped preserved ginger
1 broken cinnamon stick
25 g grated orange peel

Mix all the ingredients in a bowl. Tie one dessertspoon of mixture in a 15 cm square of pretty cotton material. Tie up tightly with ribbon, making a small sachet. Leave two long strings of ribbon. These sachets will dry out after use and can be used two or three times. They are also useful for freshening up a sick-room.

Orange Peel Room Freshener

Our family is addicted to eating oranges by the fire in winter. This is a way to use up the orange peel. It gives you sore thumbs from pushing in the cloves so just do a few at a time.

As you peel the oranges cut the peel you remove into 2 cm strips. Insert 4 or 5 whole cloves into each strip and set to dry in the warm room. Move them around as they dry and by the end of winter you will have a basket full of clove-scented orange peel and a clove-and-orange-scented room. Present the whole basket full to a bedridden friend and make yourself a new lot next winter.

SONG OF THE RAIN

Night,
And the yellow pleasure of candlelight . . .
Old brown books and the kind fine face of the clock
Fogged in the veils of the fire; its cuddling tock

The cat
Greening her eyes on the flame litten mat;
Wickedly wakeful, she yawns at the rain
Bending the roses over the pane.
And a bird in my heart begins to sing
Over and over the same sweet thing.

'Safe in the house with my boyhood's love
And our children asleep in the attic above.'

Hugh McRae

Index